THE CAMP FOLLOWER

John Reilly Taylor

PublishAmerica
Baltimore

© 2011 by John Reilly Taylor.
All rights reserved. No part of this book may be reproduced, stored in a retrieval system or transmitted in any form or by any means without the prior written permission of the publishers, except by a reviewer who may quote brief passages in a review to be printed in a newspaper, magazine or journal.

First printing

PublishAmerica has allowed this work to remain exactly as the author intended, verbatim, without editorial input.

Hardcover 978-1-4560-5524-0
Softcover 978-1-4560-5525-7
PUBLISHED BY PUBLISHAMERICA, LLLP
www.publishamerica.com
Baltimore

Printed in the United States of America

THE BEGINNING

It was 2002, I was sixty-one years old, lying on a gurney in the local hospital's intensive care unit with a doctor telling me that I had twenty minutes to live unless I was injected with a blood thinner called a clot buster; and it was successful. Of course he also pointed out that the clot buster could dissolve the clot and still cause my death. Well, it looked like I had twenty minutes or less to live. I agreed to have the clot buster and here I am, still breathing. I spent the next four days connected to a bunch of tubes unable to get out of bed. Evidentially the hospital had its own TV station because I could only get one station with a movie. They played the war movie "Midway" continuously 24 hours a day for the four days I was incarcerated in that bed. I finally got to the point where I was rooting for the Japanese because nobody could be as stupid as Charlton Heston crashing into the edge of the aircraft carrier over and over, approximately forty-eight times during my incarceration. I don't even understand why he wanted to save that busted up plane after it had been shot up that badly. While I was lying in bed I was thinking what a unique youth I had. This was of course intensified by the war movie playing 24 hours a day in the background. I'm an army brat who spent most of his childhood living in foreign places for short periods of time.

I'm kind of fatalistic about life since I've faced death at least four other times during my lifetime. That being said, I have never been to war, or even a soldier; although the first eighteen years of my life were centered about living in war zones either after a major conflict, or before one.

This story is about the unseen people who have a special personal relationship with the countries warriors and who remain outside of the public eye, but do contribute to the health of the armed forces. In other words we are the Camp Followers. I'm sure that since the time of the ancient Greeks and the Roman Empire things have been the same.

My family lived a fantastic life from the end of the Second World War to 1960. Not only did we travel and live in two-thirds of the world but my father worked for all of the top military leaders the U.S. produced during the Second World War years. If there were bombed out buildings or guerrilla skirmishes, we probably lived there. That might sound exotic, but adapting to a new culture and environment can be quite stressful. This story is of my youth and the unusual experiences I have had, coupled with my father's biographical experiences after dedicating twenty years of his life to the military and the country.

During my adult life I have told antidotal stories to my friends during conversations and they all responded to the stories telling me that I should write a book. My mother was told the same thing when she was alive. My father didn't have to consider writing because he was the lead actor in our family's saga. Dad stayed in the service after the War and had the most unusual assignments which kept him travelling. The normal army officer gets a peacetime assignment and stays there for approximately three years as a natural rotation, not us. My father was always on temporary duty assignment during the years he worked for SHAPE and its client NATO. He was either in Paris, or London, or Heidelberg, or Athens, or Istanbul, or Naples, or toward the end of his career before retirement, Viet Nam. We, the rest of the family lived in Germany, France, Italy and Viet Nam, as well as the US. We did stay in Europe for over three years just like a normal assignment, but we hardly ever saw dad. After the European experience came Viet Nam before that war started. Since Viet Nam was considered "in harms way" the tour assignments were limited to twelve months. Dad spent two tours there.

There is one other person that I am writing this for and that is my longtime friend Kalisa of Cannery Row fame. I made her a promise that I would write about my experiences on Cannery Row during the years of the late fifties and the early sixties. I agreed to do this at the celebration of her restaurant's fiftieth anniversary on Cannery Row. In the late fifties Cannery Row had not really changed since the days when John Steinbeck had written about it and it was far from being commercialized. Unfortunately, Kalisa passed away in 2009, but I do want to fulfill my promise to her.

My mother can't be forgotten; she was the anchor point of the family and had to put up with all the crap that dad's career dished out. Mom was a middle class housewife who was satisfied with cooking and the other housework. She was a bit self-conscious which limited her comfort level when it came to things she was expected to do as a field grade officer's wife in the army. She hated receiving lines; woman's clubs, playing bridge and almost anything else that she was expected to do commensurate with dad's rank. She loved to entertain the people she considered friends. If she didn't like you, you simply didn't exist. I remember once in Paris when she was angry the day after a party because she had to accompany dad to a cocktail party given by Field Marshall Montgomery. Montgomery was not the most likeable person; as a matter of fact he was an asshole. Just ask Patton. Now Montgomery was a teetotaler, so he served ice cream instead of booze at his parties. So here was mom riding across Paris with dad driving while she was trying to think of an acceptable excuse so dad could turn the car around and go home. Then she had to put up with the torture of the receiving line, chatting with people she didn't know and couldn't even get a goddamn drink.

Mom had an iron will. Her lifestyle included loneness, single parenting, constantly moving, long distance friendships, the lack of family close by, a very limited budget and the effects of life in various foreign cultures. She began to rely on alcohol as an escape. A great many army wives take that route to dull the pain of their environment. She also smoked a pack of cigarettes a day, which was normal for the times. After dad retired from the service she quit her 50 year old habit of smoking cigarettes cold turkey and moderated her drinking to the point where she would only have one screwdriver at social functions. The amazing thing is that she did not rely on supplements or outside influences to do those things. I remember one instance before I quit smoking that we were sitting together after a dinner. It had been thirty years since she quit smoking and she looked at me and said "that cigarette smells so goddamn good". Mom and my grandmother only swore if it was a last resort to get their point across.

THE CAMP FOLLOWER

Dad's specialty was finance which is the smallest corps in the Army, so there was a continuing need for this specialty. The finance corps would not be a good choice for someone with the ambition of reaching the General's Corps. One of the potential advantages of finance is that when you became a field grade officer, major or above, you were always in a staff position and more than likely report to the commanding general or his executive officer. The infantry and the other specialties, on the other hand had a surplus of manpower for the standing army after the war, so the army rotated most of the men back into civilian life. The small size of the finance corps also insured that dad would graduate into more responsible positions as his experience increased. It also meant that peacetime promotions would be slow in coming since the officers of the corps were approximately the same age. Army promotions are kind of like baseball, three strikes and you're out. Dad was passed over twice for promotion to Brigadier General and since he had twenty years of service, he was retired. Throughout his career his assignments ranged from finance officer for the Seventh Infantry Division during the Pacific Campaign of the Second World War to the Comptroller of the Military Assistance Advisory Group, Viet Nam; prior to the Gulf of Tonkin incident. He was one, if not the first, Comptroller serving in Viet Nam.

In defense of the importance of a finance corps, it must be pointed out the all wars are fought over treasure. That is the human condition. The treasure can be currency, or land, or religion. In modern times you don't see the leader of a political subdivision leading his troops into heroic battle like the European Kings during history. The finance corps collects the treasure and distributes it.

One of the things that I found out from dad was that the army was on a cash basis. Once a month accompanied by military police several millions of dollars in cash were deposited in the paymaster's safe, which was a lot of money in the forties and fifties. In the case of the Presidio of San Francisco, it was six million dollars a month. It was then handed out to the troops and I suppose the vendors under contract with the military base. Of course this didn't apply to capital expenditures.

Our family background is nothing unusual. I'm half Irish, a quarter Portuguese and a quarter mutt. As with most families there was half of the family that we were very close to and the other half not so much. My paternal grandmother was Portuguese; her parents had a ranch in the San Francisco Bay Area in what is now known as the City of San Leandro. Her father jumped ship in San Francisco Bay in 1896 or around there, so I guess you would have to consider him an illegal alien by today's standards. I never met him. I think her mother emigrated from the Azores. Hard to tell, she never learned English and I could never understand what she was saying. My paternal grandfather was Pennsylvania Dutch, whatever that means.

My maternal grandparents emigrated from Ireland to San Francisco in 1904 and 1905. My grandfather finally got accepted into the police force. He was a cop during his assigned shifts and a home builder during the rest of the day. He built all of the houses that they owned. He retired from the force in 1947. Since my grandfather was a cop, the depression had little effect on the family. Mom had a typical Irish Catholic upbringing. She never expected to be anything else but a stay at home wife and mother.

THE CAMP FOLLOWER

My father, on the other hand, was affected by the depression and after high school he joined the Civilian Conservation Corps. While he was out cutting down trees or whatever, he never talked about it; he studied to become a certified public account. I'm not sure if he considered accounting a means to a steady income during tough times or even if he considered accounting interesting. He didn't have the typical accountant's personality. Anyway, while he was cutting down trees he joined the Army Reserves. Someone in the reserves decided he was bright enough to become an officer and sent him to Officers Candidate School, and because of his experience in accounting, assigned him to the Finance Corps. After he left the Civilian Conservation Corps he had to look for a job, which was still fairly difficult to find at that time because of the depression. He did find that the Federal Bureau of Investigation needed finger print experts, so he applied for and got that job. He never told me what made him basically knowledgeable in finger printing in order to qualify for the job; but off he went to finger print school in Washington DC and was qualified as an expert. I wasn't born yet; and as a matter of fact my folks weren't even married yet, and I never thought to ask about that experience. The FBI was just ramping into service so it probably didn't have any better experienced fingerprint experts. The FBI had recently shot John Dillinger which resulted in a lot of notoriety and made the FBI important to the American culture as the lead federal law enforcement agency.

While all this was going on my parents got married in 1939, I was born at the end of January of 1941 in San Francisco.

7TH INFANTRY DIVISION

I'm not sure if dad ever worked for the FBI but in 1940 his reserve unit was called up to active duty. So, he was now a brand new second lieutenant in the re-activated Seventh Infantry Division at Fort Ord in Monterey. The boss of the outfit was General Vinegar Joe Stillwell. General Stillwell loved Fort Ord so much that he requested that after his death, his ashes be spread along the beaches of Fort Ord. I don't know if the general's ashes were ever spread along the beaches, but the beaches and sand dunes behind the beaches were a constant target for cannon, mortar and small arms fire until the Department of Defense closed the facility.

I've always found it interesting that FDR and the Congress promised the American People that we would not enter the war in Europe and the policy would be to continue isolationism, at the same time the government was preparing for the largest conflict in the countries history, which was centered in Europe. I don't believe that anyone saw the Japanese attack coming. I do believe that the US intelligence effort was nothing more than a guess by an old boy's network with a very low level of success. Oh well, that's politics. I don't think there is any question that the attack on Pearl Harbor by the Japanese resulted in the end of the depression since the manufacture of war material had to be greatly accelerated.

THE CAMP FOLLOWER

Dad had an army footlocker out in the garage which contained all of his paperwork from his career. After I had grown and moved away I went through their garage looking for my stuff that was stored there, things like I found a Nazi traffic sign in Germany which had the swastika and eagle on it, a program from the first "Jazz at the Philharmonic" concert autographed by all the headliners and some other stuff like my electric train. There were at least ten army footlockers in the garage with various things stored. That's when I found dad's special footlocker. I went through it a couple of times when he was out of town; he was a private person and probably wouldn't approve of me rummaging through his stuff. It took a while to go through all of the papers since I am somewhat of a history buff. There were orders signed by Stillwell, Patton, MacArthur, Mark Clark, Eisenhower, and finally Lieutenant General Samuel Williams, commander of MAAG Viet Nam. Most of the documents were typed on "flimsy" paper which held up very well during the sixty years they were in the garage. It was a history of the Army during the second half of the twentieth century.

When dad reached his mid-seventies he went down to the stationary store, bought a shredder, went home, sat in the garage and shredded 95 percent of the documents. Some of the documents were classified "Secret" or "Top Secret" from during the war. I guess he didn't want any of the documents to fall into enemy hands. I could hardly keep the tears back. The only things he didn't shred were some personal papers, NATO General Order No. 1 which moved the NATO headquarters from Heidelberg Germany to Paris and confirmed Eisenhower as the head of the NATO military effort and some Protocols and things.

I was too young to remember too much about the war years, although I do remember a few things during that period. My first recollection is December 7th. My mother and I used to argue about my memory for that day considering I was ten months old, we argued about it for forty years. On December 7th 1941 we went to my paternal grandparents for a Sunday visit. Anyway I was sitting in my "Taylor Tot" in the entry hall while the family was visiting. They lived about forty miles north of San Francisco, so we didn't see that much of them. I remember that well because the grandparents had a grandfather clock at the right hand side of the front door in the entry hall. I was memorized by the clocks pendulum. The radio was on and the announcer read the news bulletin that Pearl Harbor had been bombed by the Japanese and all military leaves were cancelled and all military personnel were to report to their bases. I don't remember the exact wording of the announcement but there was complete shock in the house, with the exception of me; I was still staring at the pendulum, having a good time. I probably remember that day because of the intense shock and the fear of the future in that house. The next thing that happened was that I was grabbed by one of my parents and headed toward the car. I remember that the car was yellow; I don't know if it was a coupe or a sedan and I assume that it was a Chevy since that's all they bought at that time; not that either matters. After that my memories for that day fade out, but I sincerely believe I remember that part of the day. That's it for my earliest memory and it is fuzzy. I'm sure that the rest of the day was total chaos, confusion and panic. History tells us that General Stillwell sent troops down the coast from Monterey to insure that the Japanese weren't going to invade.

THE CAMP FOLLOWER

In the previous year, 1940, dad's first assignment was to provide financial oversight and assistance for the building of Fort Ord near Monterey. Fort Ord was made the headquarters of the Seventh Division, and had been used primarily as a summer training camp for a reserve outfit; it had no permanent housing or many facilities for the Soldiers. The facility had to be up-graded to support the hundreds of thousands of men who would receive basic training there. The thing that dad took the most pride in was his participation in the design and construction of the Soldiers Club on the beach. That was General Stillwell's pet project; the general correctly realized that the Soldiers needed a top quality and somewhat luxurious place to go during their off hours, especially since their next assignment was in harms way. I'm sure there are literally hundreds of thousands of men who remember Fort Ord and the Soldiers Club, since it was a major training facility on the west coast until the end of the Viet Nam war.

I was two years old when we moved from San Francisco to a small cottage in Carmel, which is approximately twenty miles from Fort Ord. I remember the white picket fence at the front of the cottage and the floor furnace. I don't know why but I seem to remember all of the floor furnaces in the places where I've lived throughout my life. Must be the heat rising up your legs on a chilly day while you are straddling the grate of the heater.

Dad's experiences during the war are important because to ignore his experiences leaves a thirty month hole in the story and would be unfair to dad's biography. All I can do is report the history of dad's unit without much detail. The

Seventh Division was re-established as a California division from its Georgia roots; a lot of the core manpower coming from California. The majority of the staff personnel were inexperienced having just come from civilization life.

The division was re-designated as a motorized division and rumors abounded that it would be incorporated into Patton's Third Army for the Africa campaign. The training was modified to include the motorized basics and took place in the California desert. I don't remember it but I think that we moved from Carmel to San Luis Obispo for the desert training.

Now with all things army if they told you were going to an African desert, you most likely would end up at the North Pole. The Seventh Division was again re-designated as infantry and ended up close to the Arctic Circle in the Aleutian Islands. Dad did tell me about that because he ended up in the Aleutians with his tropical uniforms. Again we moved from San Luis Obispo to Carmel.

The division was ultimately assigned to General McArthur's Sixth Army prior to the invasion of Leyte. According to dad and his tent mates McArthur deserved the nickname "Dugout Doug" because there wasn't a foxhole or trench that he didn't fall in love with.

While the infantryman had rough living conditions including fox holes and trenches, the staff officers lived in six man tents. I really don't know if they had cots, but I would expect that they did. Anyway dad and five of his buddies decided to bunk together and named their tent the "Sad Shack", which I guess reflected their opinions of their circumstances. These guys stayed together throughout the war.

Dad (on right) and John M.
in front of Sad Shack

Dad was private so he wouldn't talk about the war and I was curious, I mean after all, dad and I watched "Victory at Sea" together enough times that I knew that there were a good many interesting stories cooped up in that head of his. When dad had retired the folks had parties that included the wartime inhabitants of the Sad Shack. I always wrangled an invitation. Then came the fun, I would make sure that the ex-Sad Shack personnel had glasses that were full of Scotch at all times and when the time was right ask questions. I found out the most interesting things, some of them explaining the non-condensed version of the war and something like you would see in the movies like MASH. Things like Purple Hearts given for wounds received from falling tent poles or things that happened during the division's rest and recovery periods.

The Seventh Division shipped out for the Aleutians in 1943. Mom and I moved to a vacant flat my grandparents had in San Francisco. We lived there until my grandparents got an offer for the flat. Housing in San Francisco was very sparse at that time. I guess you could ask for any reasonable rent, I don't know if my grandparents did that but my grandmother was a shrewd business woman. Then we moved in with my grandparents. I remember when my grandmother bought a new television. Of course this was years later. After the television had been delivered, I saw an ad in the paper which offered the same television for thirty dollars less. I told my grandmother and showed her the ad. It wasn't fifteen minutes until she had the store on the phone where she bought the TV and told them to get over to the house and take back their TV. They finally reduced their price by the thirty dollars and everybody lived happily after.

MacArthur Reviewing Troops

One of my favorite war stories is that dad was assigned the task of financially re-establishing the civilian government in the Aleutians. To complete his assignment he had five boxes of gold bullion which were stacked up in one corner of the Sad Shack and was guarded by Military Police who surrounded the tent. Dad and his tent mates went to bed, the next morning there was only one box of gold left in the tent. Well, I'm sure you can imagine how quickly the hue and cry went out. It was not until somebody noticed that there seemed to be more than one box on the stack that the realization surfaced that the rest of the gold had sunk into the Aleutian mud. So the gold was rescued. I know that this story is hard to believe but at least three of the survivors of the Sad Shack told me that story independently.

From a newspaper column of the time, Peter Edson of the NEA Washington Bureau wrote a column explaining the loss of manpower in the Seventh Division because of amputations as a result of frostbite during the Aleutian campaign. I don't have a clue who the NEA was but it was published in a local San Francisco newspaper. According to Edson the number of amputations equaled the number of casualties from other causes. This all resulted from a lack of cold weather uniforms, jackets and extra socks. The blame was squarely put on the War Department. I found the newspaper article while going through a box of pictures.

The Seventh Division went on to fight in Kwajalein, Leyte and Okinawa. Dad was awarded an arrowhead for his Pacific Defense metal because he was in the first wave of an invasion. He was probably in the first wave of the invasion of Leyte to be on the beach when MacArthur made his triumphant entrance

Invasion of the Philippines

to the beach as seen in the movies. MacArthur's only talking script was "I have returned" and then walk up the beach with that stupid looking pipe. According to the guys in the Sad Shack that movie is the twenty-second take of MacArthur's entrance and he had at least twenty-two pairs of pants for the film. I guess you could see that his pants were dry when he was walking down the ramp of the landing craft and on the next take, without new pants, you could see that his pants were wet. That's what they told me and they had no reason to lie. I know that MacArthur had one giant ego, but to take it to that extreme is simply unbelievable since the men he was commanding were living with their bellies on the ground.

I don't remember too much about the war years. I do remember a couple of things. I couldn't understand why we needed black-out shades on the windows so I would pull the shades away from the window to look out at night, which would instantly get me a reprimand. I think it's so interesting that the people along the West Coast could become so paranoid about a Japanese invasion. It only seems logical that the Japanese would invade Hawaii before their war machine continued to the West Coast. We had already taken back the Aleutian Islands. I guess my version of their strategy makes it evident why I didn't become a general or even go to West Point.

I got into other trouble like the time I locked myself in the bathroom and had to be rescued by the Fire Department. Being Irish the Fireman who rescued me happened to be my uncle. Then there were the outings with my grandfather where he would take me out and we would head for the Kezar Stadium Jail so that he could play Gin Rummy with the other cops and I could play in the holding cells. The only times there were prisoners in the cells was during football games and those people were just plain drunk. There were also the outings with my grandmother where we would go to Golden Gate Park and go to the Japanese Tea Gardens because it is beautiful and relaxing. I had re-named it the Chinese Tea Gardens which she thought was great and talked about for the rest of her life.

Dad had a bad habit during the war. He would collect souvenirs from the battlefields and ship them home to my grandfather. The only problem with that is he was picking up live Japanese ammunition. This stuff all got stored in my grandfather's closet. I used to touch it on occasion even though that was strictly forbidden. I remember that there was a gun camera taken from a Japanese airplane. It didn't seem to matter how big or dangerous something was, it was shipped. Then, of course, there was the "Samurai" sword. I still have it hanging in my home office. It's still as shiny and sharp as the day dad liberated it. My grandfather had a fellow cop over for some reason and showed the booty including the ammunition to him. He suggested that the bomb disposal unit be invited over at their first opportunity. That was the end of the "Funston Avenue Ammo Dump" in San Francisco.

After the surrender of the Japanese a part of the Seventh Division was assigned to Korea for police action. Dad didn't have to go since he had all of the requisites to return home. That was fortunate considering the Korean War started in 1950 and we were in Europe. If he had gone to Korea there was more than a likely chance he would be transferred back to his home division, the seventh, still in Korea and one of the first outfits to fight in the Korean conflict.

The real adventure started after dad returned home from the war. The only story I heard about dad's homecoming was that he wanted to surprise my mother so he arrived in San Francisco but didn't call to say he would be home for dinner that night. I think that mom believed that he was in Korea with the rest of the seventh. Well, because of rationing my mother fixed powered scrambled eggs and spam for dinner. Here he was looking forward to a real home cooked meal and got the same food as he had for the past thirty months.

After the excitement died down my parents started to normalize our lifestyle. There were too many people in my grandparents flat, so the first thing my folks did was find a place of their own. I don't remember too much about that except we moved into a house about twelve blocks away from my grandparents. The house was built on a sand dune so there wasn't any grass or other plants in the back yard. I remember playing in the sand with my toy trucks, eating ants. Eating the ants always got a tremendous reaction from mom. The only other thing I remember is that I took my little girlfriend for a walk to my grandparents to get some candy from my grandmother. Didn't tell anybody of course which provided the two families lots of excitement for a little while. I guess that's understandable since even then it was unusual to see two five year olds walking down the street alone. I got hell for that one. I'm so glad that my lifetime includes a period when a child could walk down the streets safely.

Anyway, my father's first assignment after the war was to be the finance officer at the Greenbrier Hotel in White Sulphur Springs West Virginia. Even then the Greenbrier was one of the most prestigious hotels in the United States. This was, of

Greenbriar Hotel converted to Ashford General Hospital

course, twenty or so years before they built the underground bunkers to house the government during nuclear war. The Greenbrier had been commandeered during the war as a military hospital and re-named the Ashford General Hospital. It was a 2,000 bed army hospital with an adjacent building to the main hotel building re-named Hotel Hart for staff living quarters; and the golf course was turned into a army golf course and Officers Club.

German Prisoners of War were housed in a camp not far from the hospital. They were used as the kitchen and serving help for the facility. I guess they performed miscellaneous services at the hospital, fought forest fires and did miscellaneous projects in the nearby communities around White Sulphur Springs. All in all they performed their jobs excellently. I guess they were paid for their efforts since they had their own Post Exchange. The internet revealed that they had their own orchestra and most of the amenities that would have been available at home. I understand from the internet that there were two prisoners who seemed to escape during a work detail, but it turns out they simply missed the bus returning to camp and had to walk back. Most of these prisoners if not all of them were captured while they were in Rommel's Afrika Corp. I know my folks fell in love with their cooking from postcards sent to my grandmother.

We took the train from San Francisco to White Sulpher Springs which was my first experience on a train. It was fun since some of the cars had observation decks and we got to sleep in the pull down beds. We stayed in the Hotel Hart and ate our meals and hung out at the golf club. I was the only five year old kid in the hotel, which made my days somewhat boring, not having any other kids to play with.

THE CAMP FOLLOWER

I did have some company other than my parents in the form of the Greenbrier's greens keeper and his wife. They were an English couple and I guess I substituted as a grandchild. They lived in a nice cottage near the hotels entry gates with their parrot. The wife would bake me cookies and I would play with the parrot, with a lot of supervision. The greens keeper took a round headed putter and converted it into a driver so that I would have my own golf club. I kept that club for many years.

Even though I was only five and much too young, dad bought me a Lionel train. The rules for the use of the train were quite simple. I couldn't use it unless dad was there and then it was a fight to see who was going to run the train. You can imagine how many times I won the argument. I recall that the most important job I was given was to put the smoke pellet into the stack, of course I couldn't light it. That's when I learned that if you have a kid, you can use the kid as an excuse to buy and play with things that you're too old for and that you really wanted when you were a kid, without criticism from your peer group. I've used that in my later life. Wives always seem to catch on to that scam.

The next thing I remember about the Greenbrier is more serious. My folks and I went to the swimming pool. I was in the pool in the shallow end and was told to hang onto the handhold at the side of the pool. I even got the "don't move" command while mom was telling me that they were going to swim to the other end and back. Of course, I decided to join them. I was inching my way down the side of the pool planning my big surprise when for some unknown reason I let go of the side of the pool. I think someone bumped me. I was later told that the lifeguard noticed a tuff of hair floating in the pool and pulled it out. The next thing I remember is being in the men's locker room with a forest of hairy legs surrounding me and coughing up water. You might think that my folks were inattentive to me, but I can assure you that I may have been the first army "brat" who truly deserved that title. I simply did what I wanted to do regardless of the consequences. The rest of my youth had many more of these situations, but I'm still here at age 69.

The last thing I remember happening at the Greenbrier makes me laugh since for all practable purposes my mother racially integrated the Greenbrier before Truman integrated the military services. My mother was not going to let the upcoming Easter be ruined by the lack of children for her sons Easter egg hunt. So, she went into White Sulphur springs and invited all of the children's parents she could find. She organized the whole thing, having the hotel kitchen staff color the eggs; and the lobby staff hide them. I remember my companion during the egg hunt was a little black girl. I don't think we collected all the eggs before the hunt ended. Now the hotel couldn't do anything about it except complain to the army about their "separate but equal" policy as the hotel was a temporary federal facility, and the army couldn't do anything about because of its own bureaucy. We didn't know anything about segregation, you never heard of it in the neighborhood where we lived in San Francisco, nor was it ever discussed within the family.

The army decided that dad needed to go to what I think was a war college at Fort Knox Kentucky. We got temporary quarters on the base; the next door neighbor was an English army officer attending school there. They had a son my age so I had someone to play with. I do remember that this was my first experience with icy sidewalks. I think that I still hold the record of slipping on an ice covered sidewalk onto my ass and getting the seat of my pants dirty and wet from the slush. I finally learned how to navigate the icy sidewalks in an upright position. The one exception happened many years later when I was meeting our corporate lawyer for dinner in Chicago. Here I was dressed in a three piece suit with a good overcoat and fell on my ass again. All of the people around me tried to help me up which resulted in a pretty good case of embarrassment.

SIXTH ARMY

After my father completed the school he was transferred back to San Francisco to the Sixth Army Headquarters. We were going home! Again we took the train and we even got a sleeping compartment.

When we got home we found out that we had quarters on the Presidio itself. I still consider that house home. It was the first time that we had lived as a family in a house with grass in the yard and I was already six years old. I had my own bedroom and there was a basement in which dad had set up a woodshop so that he could build furniture as a hobby. It was in a section of the Presidio known as Infantry Terrace, as a matter of fact the house number is 336. It's still there and people are living in it, I guess renting it from the National Park Service. There were forests behind the house and a canyon in the shape of a bowl in the front. The shape of the row of houses was a horseshoe. The inner part of the horseshoe was filled with wildlife. My favorites were the quail which used the area as a breeding ground. Italian Prisoners of War took care of the lawns; it was kind of interesting to see these guys with the POW painted on the backs of their shirts. I don't know why these guys weren't repatriated, it was 1947. Maybe they just didn't want to go home. At the front of the terrace across the street was the main post theater where my friends and I paid ten cents on Saturday mornings to watch cartoons and episodes of Roy Rogers all morning. Roy was my hero.

My next experience with water occurred when after a Boy Scout meeting. Mom, who was the troop leader in the absence of dad, took the troop to the beach for a late days outing. I was dressed in my school uniform: corduroy pants, shirt and tie, and a cotton sweater. I took off my shoes and went wading. The undertow caught me and pulled me down into the surf. I was being washed into the bay. I dug my hands into the sand and tried to hang on. The surf was so strong that that before I knew it my arms were in the sand up to my elbows. My arms didn't work that well as anchors because I was still slowly moving out to sea. Mom started yelling for a surf fisherman to help. My grandmother had come with us and both of the women were hysterical. The fisherman came over and ultimately pulled me to safety. I guess that was number two of my close calls.

Another thing we did was go down to the Army Air Force Base at Crissey Field and fish off the dock. Crissey Field was a runway where Piper Cubs could land for observation flights. I don't think we were supposed to fish there or probably even be on that part of the Presidio. Of course all of the fish were too small to eat so the whole experience was wasted, but it was something to do during the afternoon. My fiend and I had good time fishing; I think that his name was Shawnasey. That brings up another point about growing up in the service. You meet so many people who are in and out of your life during such a short period of time that you can't remember them.

It was a short walk from Crissey Field to North Point. North Point was an old fort left over from I guess the Russians or the Spanish. It sits right under the South Anchor of the

Golden Gate Bridge. It was a multiple story fort which was fun and scary to play in. It had been used during the Civil War to guard the entrance of San Francisco Bay. I think at the time it was closed to the public but we sure had fun in it. The only problem with playing in the cells and cannon ports was the wind blowing through the golden gate could get kind of cold and very strong. Anyway it made it more fun since we weren't supposed to be there in the first place.

Off the main road near the house, I can't remember the name of the road, was what I guess was an obstacle course with a large log tower in it. I guess that the soldiers were made to climb up to get their training. That was the place we could go and play hooky from school and smoke cigarettes. We had a good time there but I don't remember any of us scaling the log structure. The area was completely surrounded by forest so there was little chance of anyone discovering us.

Since we were Catholic and mostly Irish I was enrolled in Saint Bridget's school at the corner of Broadway and Van Ness. It was about thirty blocks from the Presidio and I took a bus from the house to school. I remember one day I boarded the bus and all of my compatriots started to chant "Herman the German" to the bus driver who was named Herman. Germans were not that popular after the war in the area. I don't really remember joining in but I'm sure I did. Anyway I got home that afternoon and the front door to the house was locked. That was the door that I usually came through when getting home. I rang the bell and in a couple of minutes mom opened the front door, looked at me and slapped my face telling me that I would never insult anyone again. That impressed me to the point that I didn't insult anyone for a long time. There were other punishments of course. The most notable was my dad's army belt. If you're not familiar with an army belt of the time it was a woven belt with a brass buckle on one end and a brass tab on the other. Dad carefully explained to me that the belt had three levels of punishment, the doubled up belt was the minimum punishment, the brass tab the next step and the buckle the most serious punishment. He also explained that if the punishment was required I would have to go to the basement, wait for him and take my punishment. It only happened a couple of times but I can assure you that I started crying while I was waiting for him in the basement and I really meant it when I said I would be good forever in the future. Luckily the worst offence I committed was the doubled up belt.

Then there was the occasion when I was kept after school. The nun who was my teacher had good reason to keep me after school. I can't remember what I did but I'm sure she was correct in her decision. Anyway when she released me I went out to the bus stop in time to see the bus leaving the bus stop. So now I am thirty blocks from home with all of my money spent on my lunch. I was homeless! Things like a little adversity like that never stopped me before so I started to hike the thirty blocks to get home. I didn't walk down Van Ness. I took another street which had me outside of a search route. I finally got home to my folks who were more than a bit worried about me. I had to promise that I wouldn't do that again. I think I said before that I was lucky to have lived in San Francisco during the period when a kid could walk down the streets safely. Presently you see second graders like myself in herds crossing the street.

Dad's boss was General Mark Clark, who he sincerely liked. The general had multiple reputations that were opposed to one another. One called him a guy with the personality of a cold fish; Eisenhower and General Marshall regarded him as one of the best troop commanders in the Army with an emphasis on training. Later the general was transferred to Korea for that war effort. I guess that was after Truman fired MacArthur.

I did like the regimen that the Presidio and the army afforded with its structure for all the normal things in life. You could always tell what time it was either at retreat or taps, or if you were a morning person reveille, I wasn't.

An army post in those days was separated from the civilian community, for example, the officers club had slot machines installed in the bar; while in San Francisco you could get arrested for even having a slot machine.

To my great delight every once in a while the troops would parade on the parade ground with the full Presidio band. It made you really proud to be associated with such a fine organization. Look at me talk, I was supposed to go to West Point, and so I did everything I could to disqualify myself. When dad decided to send me off to the army as an enlisted man, I refused. Dad didn't talk to me for six months after that. By that time I had twenty years in and around the army. I also knew that a major war was imminent in Viet Nam and I really thought that if I went there, I wouldn't be coming back. Besides I had already been to Viet Nam.

SUPREME HEADQUARTERS ALLIED POWERS EUROPE

In 1949 dad got orders assigning him to the European Command (EUCOM) in Heidelberg Germany. He went out and bought a new 1949 Buick so that we would have a decent ride across the US, and he could make some money on the car by selling it when we got to Europe. Dad's orders were delayed for some reason until January 1950. We took the southern route since we were travelling during the winter. This was the start of my great adventure even though I had been out of California before; this would be the first time we would be driving and the difference of being five and eight years old is monumental. This, of course, was before Eisenhower led the effort to build a national highway system. We were going to travel south down California to the intersection of Route 66 and then cross the US, finally heading north through the Smoky Mountains and Appalachia to New York City. We would then board a ship and cross the Atlantic.

The entertainment we had available for the trip were the radio plays. Didn't matter how old you were, your life experiences compensated for your age and permitted you to experience the play in a way you found acceptable in your own mind. With the exception of real life history or news, or nature, or science; television offers nothing. Those radio plays kept the trip across the country fresh. My father would actually drive into the night, without complaint, so that we could listen to the plays and when they were over for the night pull into a motel. During the days we would look at the interesting things in the scenery and played "Twenty Questions" when we got bored. Of course our favorite was the Burma Shave signs. We would watch for them by the side of the road and then one of us would read them aloud, then laugh and laugh. We were all entertained throughout the trip and probably had more family fun during that trip then any other time in our family relationship. I got to eat anything I wanted within reason, so twice a day I would have a cheeseburger, fries and a chocolate milkshake from a Howard Johnson's if there was one in the town we were passing through. Occasionally I could have a banana split if we found a place that made a good one. I was in kid heaven.

I don't remember the sequence of the radio plays but I do remember our favorites. We would listen to Amos and Andy, Fiber Magee and Molly, "Gangbusters", "Inner Sanctum" and last but not least Jack Benny.

The trip from San Francisco to Los Angeles was uneventful and boring especially for an eight year old. The trip began to get more interesting when we entered the Painted Desert. Dad had to convince me that the petrified trees were real trees that had turned to rocks instead of just being strange rocks. As I remember we saw some dinosaur fossils, but I'm not sure where. New Mexico was about the same as Arizona. We stopped occasionally at Indian communities. Now we were getting to Texas where everything there is supposed to be big. As we were driving up to the agricultural station on the Texas state line I noticed a sign on the lawn saying "Keep off the Grass". Now you would think that for the pride of the state the government would have insured that green grass was growing in some part of the state adjacent to a highway. Nope, not a blade of green grass anywhere along the roads in Texas. It's funny I can remember that sixty years later.

Dad did make a strategic error when he mentioned that we had just passed the western boundary of the King Ranch which I think was the largest ranch in the US at that time. Anyway it was a perfect chance to make my backseat presence known by asking him every few minutes if we were still on the King Ranch. He showed very unusual patience and answered me. He finally lied to me and told me that we had passed the eastern boundary a few minutes ago.

I guess in retrospect it was easier to humor me than to start a war which would have been inevitable if the folks had been more stringent.

Another thing in Texas that was interesting was that I saw a bunch of men walking on the top of a berm in a single file with one guy leading the way on a horse. I asked dad about it and he told me it was a chain gang and those guys in the line were chained together. That blew my mind because I was used to the Italian Prisoners of War mowing the lawns at the Presidio. They didn't need to be chained and only needed a couple of bored looking MP's to guard them, and the MP's were there for show more than anything else. I didn't realize that the Italians were probably trying to immigrate to the US. Why would they be in a hurry to go back to a war torn Italy.

The Smokey Mountains were fantastic; the tops of the mountains were shrouded in a blue haze with giant forests. I am starting to get a little tired of travelling in the car.

We finally boarded the "Henry Gibbins" and settled into our staterooms. I had never been on a ship like this before. The Gibbins was an army transport ship and I'm sure had army troops somewhere on it but I didn't see them, or maybe I just don't remember them. We had regular staterooms with two berths in each stateroom. The ship did have a few other kids my age and lots of passageways so I could see that this was going to be a fun trip. I never had such a big play toy as this. It even had a ships store where given enough change; I could have a candy bar or gum between meals.

The only problem that I personally had was the fact that my birthday was in a couple of days and I had already been told that we were going to celebrate it after we got to Germany. In retrospect how can you deny that this is probably your most important birthday if you're having it in the middle of the Atlantic Ocean and going to a new exciting life?

As we left the dock, it seems that all of the passengers were at the side of the ship just like in the movies. Everyone was waving to the people on the dock. Then we passed the Statue of Liberty. The people at the rail became quiet. Mom started crying. We were leaving the US for a foreign port that no one was familiar with, and after a major war to boot.

U.S. Army Transport Henry Gibbins

We were heading for the north Atlantic, the place where the Titanic had sunk. The ship was joined by a school of Porpoise or Dolphin, don't know which. They entertained us for a couple of hours. As you would expect the north Atlantic in January is not calm. The ship's bow would disappear into a coming wave and then break out spraying seawater all over the bow of the ship. I would stand just outside of the hatch leading to the bridge, hanging on to the rail and watch the power of the waves and the ability of the ship to survive.

The next couple of days brought the flying fish. It was a little difficult for me to understand that if the fish couldn't fly, they would get eaten. Their flight seemed to be random, they would take off at the top of a swell and travel a couple hundred yards.

Speaking of eating, the ship had the best food you could imagine. Every table had a large bowl of fresh fruit on it, guess that was to prevent scurvy, but I doubt if scurvy could develop in ten days. Since you didn't have the opportunity to select anything not on the menu, my cheeseburger, french fries and chocolate milkshake were out of the question, until we got back to dry land.

My birthday arrived and I was mentally ready for the delay of any celebration and especially birthday presents. Imagine my surprise when I was ushered into the folk's stateroom and presented with three packages. I tore into the packages and found a Boy Scout pocket knife with a piece of wood for whittling and a Boy Scout hatchet complete with a belt sheath. The third package contained a Kodak Brownie camera

The North Atlantic

complete with film. The camera was the most useful; I was now nine years old, on a ship crossing the Atlantic Ocean with a brand new camera. After learning from dad how to load the film and take a picture, I turned to the jack knife with the only instruction being never cut anything with the knife blade moving toward you. Of course you know the ultimate result. I was cutting my piece of wood with the blade moving toward me, the knife slipped and cut open my thumb. Off I went to mom with the blood dripping down my thumb and tears in my eyes. As she was wrapping my thumb, she carefully explained that if I was going to do adult things, I had to act like an adult. The scar is still visible and I am still quite proud of it, I consider it my dueling scar. I was now on my way to manhood.

After the flow of blood subsided I turned my attention to the camera. Dad had loaded a roll of film into the camera and I went out to take pictures of the most interesting thing on the ship. In my mind that could only be one thing and that was the waves breaking over the bow of the ship. I don't know if it's a character flaw in me, but I really had no interest in taking pictures of people, besides nobody was on deck and the camera didn't have a flash unit. That camera was a good friend to me and lasted throughout Europe and well into my early teens. It finally developed a light hole in the plastic and refused to take any more pictures. I can honestly say that it had a tough life.

The rest of the trip was pretty mundane except for the lifeboat drills. They were fun and it all centered about putting on those overstuffed life preservers and finding our way to the lifeboat station. My life preserver was so large that I could hardly see over the stuffing. I always wanted to get into one of the lifeboats but thought better of it.

Arriving in Bremerhaven

We were one day from docking at Bremerhaven Germany. The last shipboard dinner was excellent and we were all looking forward to disembarking from the ship into this new land, to us anyway.

There were probably five of us nine year olds that hung out together on the ship and we decided to do something I still feel guilty about. The German tugboats had pulled up alongside of the ship and was guiding her to the dock. Meanwhile our gang was at the ships rail yelling "Hey Krut, what ya doing? The war was over and we had no business yelling any names at anyone, much less adults. It's a good thing that mom didn't find out about that. That would have deserved a slap in the face, and it wouldn't have been the first time that I got that slap.

We disembarked from the ship and waited for the car to be unloaded. Even though I don't remember we must have stayed in a hotel in Bremerhaven that night. Logic tells me that we couldn't get the car after it was unloaded, fill it with the suitcases and boxes, and then drive to Mannheim in time for lunch. I'm guessing that the next day we took off for Mannheim and arrived there in the early afternoon. Mannheim had been carpet bombed by the English Air Force. There wasn't too much standing. The hotel was half gone, it had two elevators, one in operating condition and the other a one-way express down. The only thing that was left was half the elevator shaft.

The next morning dad drove to Heidelberg to make sure that our quarters were ready for us to move into the next day, and to sign the furniture inventories. To save time and expedite the movement of military personnel, the army furnished most of the housing with decent furniture. This required an inventory to insure that the army officers weren't stealing from the army. Our personal possessions, with the exception of clothing and small appliances, were in storage in the states. Mom and I decided to spend the afternoon in the hotel room since the only sights in Mannheim were of bombed out buildings. It was lunch time and we were in the hotel so we decided on room service. Mom suggested that we have a cheeseburger, fries and a milkshake. That sounded really great to me especially after all of the nourishing food we ate on the ship. The hotel kitchen didn't know how nor did they have the equipment to make a milkshake. They did know how to make French fries, and the cheeseburgers were something else. The kitchen topped the hamburger with the only cheese they had, Limburger. We ate the French fries and drank a bottle of Coke.

We were amazed by the number of older people including women who were clearing rubble from the bombed out buildings. They were clearing the buildings by hand since there was no heavy equipment available and the danger of unexploded munitions and dead bodies. There weren't many younger men around; I'm guessing that they had not been released from the POW camps, especially from the Russian front. The Berlin Airlift was over and there was a nervous peace between us and the Russians. You could tell that the Germans wanted to salvage what they could and start the rebuilding effort. The Marshall Plan was starting to kick in which made rebuilding cost effective, and strengthened the economy of both Germany and the US. The US was selling a lot of equipment and material to the Europeans. For example one of the best going concerns there during this period was the Caterpillar Equipment Co.

It was dinner time, dad had gotten back from Heidelberg and someone had recommended a restaurant a half a block away. We walked from the hotel to the restaurant which was in the basement of a bombed out building. The atmosphere and the food were excellent, and they didn't have Limburger cheese. The restaurant made me uncomfortable, I guess it was just the idea that above our heads was a huge mountain of rubble that used to be buildings, and could have contained unexploded bombs and dead bodies.

We now had possession of the house in Heidelberg, at least on paper. The address of the house was Im Gabelacker 7. The next morning we drove to Heidelberg. It was an amazing ride; we were going from a place that had seen a major war that destroyed everything in its path to a place where there had been no war in centuries. The Neckar River ran through the town with an ancient gated bridge guarding the town, a large castle sitting on the side of a mountain, an ancient university and cobblestone streets. There was also a church that I was told was fought over by the Catholics and Protestants during the Reformation. The church walls had to be supported by wooden logs on a diagonal from the ground to the tops of the walls. Without the support the walls would have fallen over. There were the famous honey wagons carrying fertilizer to the fields, and of course we were warned that the vegetables had to be disinfected before we could eat them.

The house was neat; it was a middle class house with enough bedrooms so that we could have a live-in housekeeper. The best thing was that there was a large Black Cherry tree in the backyard; I could stay in it all day long if I wanted too. Of course during the cherry season I had the opportunity to sit in the tree if there was nothing else going on and eat cherries until I got sick.

THE CAMP FOLLOWER

I needed an ID card and Dog Tags. I'm not quite sure why I needed the Dog Tags but I got the regular army Dog Tags that all of the soldiers had with the exception that mine pointed out that I was a dependant instead of having a serial number. I wore those things until I came back to the states after leaving Viet Nam. I could see their value in Viet Nam, but it would have taken World War III to be of any use in Europe. Maybe it was for kidnapping or accidents or something.

The next thing was entertainment. The only station we had available in English was the AM broadcast of AFN "Armed Forces Network". It carried US national and German news, as well as, news from the individual army units stationed in Europe, but for me, it carried "Your Hit Parade" as well as baseball games. Every year we were in Europe dad would bet me one dollar, my weekly allowance, on the NY Yankees in the World Series. Since in the years of 1950 to 1953 the series was won by the Yanks, dad always recovered some of my allowance with great glee.

Mom got a recommendation for a housekeeper. Elsie was about nineteen years old, could really cook and was very clean. She had a very cheerful disposition and was quickly adopted by the family. One day she decided to show me how to make wine. There was a hedge made up of current berry bushes between our driveway and the driveway to the adjacent house. Elsie and I carefully collected the berries, found some empty wine bottles, cleaned them out real well, crushed the berries and put the berries and sugar into the bottles. Then the bottles went into the kitchen pantry to ferment. In a couple of days Elsie and I were getting hell from mom because during the night she was awakened by systematic explosions in the kitchen pantry. Mom made us clean it up from ceiling to the floor; we never wanted to make wine again. Current juice is a nice shade of red.

Mom bought a can of shredded coconut in the gallon size. A friend and I opened it in the basement and started eating. We ate so much of it that we were stuffed with coconut. My friend finally went home and the can had a great deal of coconut left. Now being taught that I was expected to be a member of the "clean plate club" and for the sake of the "starving children in China" I attempted to finish the can. Needless to say it was twenty years before I ate anything with coconut in it.

Next came school, I was enrolled in Mrs. Swanson's third grade class. I loved Mrs. Swanson. The school system and Mrs. Swanson had the opportunity to immerse us in the German culture and the history of Heidelberg. We went on field trips to the castle and the university and all of the monuments that were available. Heidelberg was pristine, so much so that there were rumors that the allies didn't bomb it because they wanted to use the town for the EUCOM headquarters. The army refuted the rumor, but you never know. The army's explanation was that there were no military installations in Heidelberg so bombing was unnecessary.

The folks decided that I needed a belated birthday gift. All of the other kids were riding bikes and I was afoot. So dad and I went down to the bike shop where I was given a choice between a couple of bikes. The one I choose was deep metallic red in color with silver lettering and a running greyhound on the front fender. It took a little while until I convinced dad that it was the bike for me. I now had a basic bike, no gearing or anything but good looking wheels. Normal German bikes were painted black and really not very sexy. Being handy with my hands I was already plotting for gearing and large sprocket derailleur in the future.

The Germans were desperate for basic food items that were strictly rationed. These items included flour, sugar, butter, coffee, tea and cigarettes. The black market was established to barter those supplies for heirlooms owned by the Germans and included household services. The Germans had a system of marking some part of the house with a sign to let other black marketers know that particular house was a house you could do business with. I don't think that the authorities were ever really interested in breaking up the black market because of its positive effects on the economy. Besides can you see a general telling his wife that she couldn't barter on the black market again? Hell at nine years old I had a cigarette ration at the Post Exchange of a carton a week and that meant that I had purchasing power even though I never got to use it. Mom bartered for many antiques during our stay in Heidelberg. My portrait was painted in oils for a couple of cartons of cigarettes and some sugar by an accomplished portrait artist. There was even a shop in Mannheim that took the antiques on consignment and re-sold them. Most of the American women knew of the shop and utilized it. It was raided once by the MP's and German Police but I don't think they did anything.

Then came Willie. Willie showed up on the front doorstep one day looking for day labor. Elsie opened the door for him and introduced him to mom. Turns out that Willie had been in a Russian Prisoner of War camp for at least a year. He was severely emaciated, must have weighed ninety pounds. He had walked and hitched rides from Russia to Heidelberg. Well, the women of the house sprang into action with mom making Willie comfortable in the kitchen so he and Elsie could talk, and Elsie cooked a meal for him. Mom called dad to see if there was anything we could do for Willie. Dad suggested that if Willie would accept it, he could become our fireman. We had a coal fired central heating system and of course someone had to provide oversight while the coal was being unloaded from the delivery truck, clean the coal from around the coal bin, as well as. feeding the furnace. The next thing was Willie's living quarters. There was a semi finished room in the basement, so dad gave Willie the building materials and he could build anything he wanted. Willie had simple tastes and I'm sure that a curtain that would close would be an improvement over the POW camp. An equitable wage was settled on by dad and Willie, which I'm sure was generous. I nailed up a horse shoe over Willie's door to show my comfort having Willie around. Willie turned it around because I nailed it in the down position where the luck would run out. Dad and Willie built a brick barbecue pit in the backyard; I think it was the only one in Heidelberg. Willie also did the general maintenance around the house. We truly were living an idyllic life.

Dad had found a buyer for that big beautiful black Buick. As a replacement for the Buick dad bought a Morris Minor. Now for anyone who is familiar with a Morris Minor I'm sure they would ask why. It's a small exaggeration to say that you could cut the top of the passenger compartment off the Buick and fit the whole Morris Minor into that passenger compartment. Nobody had any room for their legs which became very evident later on. Dad wore the steering wheel between his chest and his knees.

My time was spent with my friends biking around Heidelberg and the adjacent countryside. The countryside was fun because of the honey wagons and the abundance of crops in the fields. Sticking playing cards next to the bikes wheels so that they would rattle like a machine gun was the in thing to do. The combination of the cards and the cobblestones were better than simply having the cards alone since you had the noise and the bumpiness from the cobblestones. Home base, of course, was the Cherry tree. I could make it up into that tree in about thirty seconds. If there were cherries I would take a box or bag with me and pick enough for the whole family.

A friend of mine and I were riding our bikes down town when we noticed a beautiful horse drawn hearse. The horses were entirely black and the hearse was a dark wood with glassed in panels all around giving good visibility to the casket. Inside the hearse were all kinds of American appliances including a one eyed monster. My friend knew what it was and told me it was a television set. He explained what it did, which amazed me that it could do something like that; and that my friend even knew what it was.

Heidelberg had an Olympic sized public swimming pool which kept us kids busy when the weather was nice. Germans love to swim so the pool was always crowded. Heidelberg had all of the American amenities including a first class hospital, commissary, post exchange, theaters and the American school system. The school system had to be the best in American occupied Germany simply by the numbers of American general officers stationed there.

Ever since I can remember I have loved music. I listened to Slaughter on Tenth Avenue, Porgy and Bess and Ravel's Bolero; as well as the big bands all of the time in the Presidio. My folk's even trusted me to use the record player by myself which I took advantage of. Not only did I like classical and big band, but I also liked kid's music, my favorite was Tex Ritter's "Big Rock Candy Mountain", I still have the record. I acquired a taste for jazz later and Rock and Roll much later. I even remember listening to Bill Haley and the Comets when they first came out. Anyway mom thought that I might have had some talent and arranged for piano lessons. There was a piano in the house. Dad decided that he wanted to have piano lessons too, so the poor teacher had both of us the same day. Both of us had large fingers and had problems moving around the keyboard. Actually dad was a better student than I was, at least he learned to play "Lady of Spain" albeit badly. That's the only piece he ever played. Nobody could get me to practice. I'm sure that when mom told the teacher that the lessons weren't working out, he probably celebrated at the closest beer hall.

We did get to take one trip while we were in Heidelberg. We went to Garmish and stayed at the Hotel on Reisersee Lake. The hotel was taken over after the war for the use of the American military and their dependants. It is located by the side of the lake which in turn looks out onto the Zugspitze, which is the highest mountain in Germany. In the winter the area is a world class skiing area and in the summer it is the most fantastic alpine environment you can find. Dad and I fished for trout in the lake in the morning, caught some and took them to the kitchen in the hotel, where they prepared them for our breakfast. Some artists got permission to paint and sell their work at the wall along the lakefront. We bought two paintings from there from notable artists. One of the paintings that the folks bought was painted by an artist who gave Eisenhower painting lessons and went over to England to tutor Churchill in a painting he was doing.

Dad's assignment in Heidelberg was the most confusing, not only was the American army there but the English and

Paddling on the Reisersee

French were there also. Now the French weren't going to let the Americans run the whole thing. Nor was Montgomery for that matter.

Eisenhower had put his uniform back on and returned from the U.S. He had become the Army Chief of Staff when General George Marshall retired after the Japanese surrender and then went on to become the President of Columbia University. Dad was assigned to EUCOM but worked for the Supreme Headquarters Allied Expeditionary Forces (SHAEF). SHAEF then became Supreme Headquarters Allied Powers Europe, SHAPE. That whole SHAEF/SHAPE thing is kind of confusing. The internet stated that SHAEF turned into SHAPE in 1947, but the banner above the unit patch on dad's uniform said SHAEF for the first couple of months we were in Germany and then changed to SHAPE.

Dad's assignment was as the Deputy Chief of the Budgeting Office working for a NATO supplied Frenchman. I don't know if the Frenchman was military or civilian, but dad got along with this guy very well and the guy even gave dad a written commendation as well as making dad his assistant. Dad was a Lieutenant Colonel at the time so the commendation was important. I think his assignments ranged from oversight for consistency of the English and French budgeting process as it related to NATO; to establishing budget methodology for the new countries joining NATO like Greece and Turkey.

In 1951 it was decided to move the NATO Headquarters from Heidelberg to Paris. Mom was having problems with her back. She had a slipped disk in the cervical region of her spine and was hospitalized at the army hospital in Heidelberg. The

House outside Paris

family was expected to join dad in Paris. Dad went to Paris to find suitable housing. A top army neurosurgeon performed surgery on mom's back. She was hospitalized for quite a while which necessitated dad's orders be extended on a humanitarian basis. Dad found some housing for us in Paris; we loaded up the Morris Minor and took off. I don't think mom enjoyed that trip. She was recently out of the hospital, still in pain, and was going from a medical team that she had confidence in into the unknown. It's a damn good thing that Europe is not that big and there aren't any really long distance trips.

We were travelling to Paris. I wasn't too excited about it since we would be riding in the Morris Minor and I loved Heidelberg, especially my cherry tree. Dad had found us a Chateau in a small village outside of Paris named Verrieres le Busson. I don't think that there was much, a guess you would call it regular housing, available. Verrieres le Busson was a typical French village. It was kind of neat; it had a long sloping hill going from the outskirts to a park in the center of the village which contained a lake. The house was run down not that it mattered to the Owner since American pigeons were renting it. There was a large aviary behind the house. The owner removed all of the birds when we moved in because he was afraid that we would kill his birds. At least that's what dad said. Of course he didn't move them out when there was a German army infantry company bivouacked on the grounds during the German occupation.

The grounds were quite large with a circular driveway starting from the front double iron gates to the house and surrounding a lawn area. The front of the house had a large glassed-in sun room with the formal living area behind that.

THE CAMP FOLLOWER

The kitchen was a French farm style kitchen with hanging pots and pans and a large stove, something like you would imagine Julia Child using. The place was really run down; as I remember my bedroom was just plain falling apart. The Owner didn't do anything to improve the place but he was there to pick up his $1,000 a month rent; in 1951 dollars. Just to give you the relative value of that $1,000 a month rent, you could buy a new American car for a little over $2,500 in the U.S.

Now the things that were wrong with the joint outweighed the things that made it livable. First I would not brush my teeth in my bathroom while we were living there. The water that came out of my bathroom lavatory stank as if it had been flushed from the toilet into a holding tank and then pumped back to my water supply. Living there was kinda like being in one of those campy English comedies.

Each bedroom had its own fireplace and the place was cold. I never wanted a fire in my fireplace because of the work hauling the wood upstairs, lighting the fire, the ash and hot coals that migrated into the room and all the other problems you have with a fireplace.

The German Soldiers that were bivouacked on the grounds must have not had a good trash removal group. Along the outside fence line were animal bones that had been picked clean. The bones were not readily evident since they were in the bushes adjacent to the concrete wall that acted as a fence. I have always assumed and hoped that the bones belonged to cattle or horses. The grounds were full of wild animals like Hedge Hogs and other wild things to pick the bones clean. I even had a Hedge Hog that I made a pet. It's hard to pet a Hedge Hog. *Sorry.*

Else had come from Germany with us to take care of the house and cook. After a couple of months she decided that she was sick of France, homesick for Germany, missed her boyfriend and was going home. Else's decision would have far reaching consequences for the family since I think that everyone wanted to go with her.

Willie had been offered a job with the people who took over the house in Heidelberg. Willie was such a gentleman and had so much class that I can only hope that the rest of his life was as successful as we tried to make it when we were in the picture.

We got to Paris during the school's summer recess, so my folks didn't have to worry about my going to school. Actually there were no English speaking schools in the area which meant that there were few options, the most feasible going to a boarding school.

It wasn't all bad in France, I had my own regimen. First thing in the morning I would get my bike out and pedal up to the bakery at the top of the hill. I would get a loaf of bread and some Croissants. And then the mad dash down the hill with the hot bread, going fast enough to prevent the bread from assuming a horseshoe shape because it was resting on my shoulder.

We did go out sightseeing and went to Versailles, the Eiffel Tower and other points of interest. I remember that we were going to the Eiffel Tower when we hailed a cab. We told the cab driver that we wanted to go to the tower which you cold see in the distance. He responded by pointing to the tower and told us we should walk. He kicked us out of his cab.

Another experience that mom had was that dad asked her to pick up a round of Camembert cheese while she was in Paris. Mom didn't know that Camembert had a unique odor and that odor was pervasive. She was riding around in taxicabs wondering what stank so badly. She couldn't seem to get away from the smell. It finally dawned on her that it was the cheese. Dad's explanation for the odor was that the cheese maker ripened the cheese under a pile of horse manure. I don't know if that was factual or not, but it did evoke a reaction from mom.

I did meet a kid who lived on the other side of the lake and was a little older than me. The family was French but had lived in New York for awhile. His parents decided to move back to France after the war. He was very talented classical violinist. Mom would hire him to play anytime they had an important dinner or cocktail party. That was always a bone of contention between mom and me. The kid would tell me that he was only going to play because of our friendship and then mom would pay him and I would lose my temper. At ten I just didn't understand the culture.

There were two English ladies next door. Their Chateau was in much better condition than ours, but then they were in some way related to the peerage in England. They were spinsters and had lived together for many years. I met one of them at the fence between the properties. She introduced herself and we got into a conversation in keeping with a ten year olds vocabulary and intellect. She told me that they were supplementing their income raising mink and ermine. Now that peaked my interest. She invited me over for tea in the afternoon. Not being sure what tea was I told mom that I had a chance to go over there for tea. My grandmother, being a proper Irish lady, had entertained the Catholic nuns from the convent across the street from my grandparent's house with high tea on a regular basis, and mom had always been an anglophile. Mom recommended that I change clothes. I was starting to feel a little less sure about this encounter. Mom convinced me that it would be fun and it was, with the exception of the tea. The cookies were good and I think that I ended up with juice as a drink. It was neat in their living room, they had a large fireplace with a fire in it and the room was warm and cozy. Later they showed me the mink cages, nasty little things. I guess you can understand their positions if you know you were going to be killed and skinned. I went over to their house a couple more times before we moved.

The other person I came across in France was an English kid whose father was an English Baron or something. Anyway they lived in the traditional family palace on the side of a hill. The only problem that they had was that the father was broke and had to rent the bedrooms in the palace to the French. Another perfect example for an English campy movie.

Our entertainment at that time consisted of a phonograph, we couldn't get AFN on the normal AM radio and we didn't have a shortwave radio. So we had to find records that we would enjoy. One of the favorite records was a record with the song "Here comes Peter Cottontail" That song was played so often that you could listen to it for a couple of times and then it would follow you in your head until you went to sleep that night.

THE CAMP FOLLOWER

The end was coming for our French experience, it was getting close to the school year. One day my folks came to me with all smiles and happiness and trying to put on the happiest face they could come up with. They asked me "How would you like to go to a boy's school in Switzerland?" Now that sounded pretty neat. I thought about it for a couple of minutes and then remembered the ads for military schools in the back of the National Geographic magazine. I asked one question "This is not a military school is it?" Dad answered with enthusiasm "with uniforms and everything". My little internal voice screamed "hell no". In a later life that would have been said as "Hell no, I won't go".

Mom sent dad out on a little errand; find quarters in Germany with a good American school that we can move into immediately. Nobody liked living in France; mom hated shopping for meat at least that was the major compliant. At the local butchers you always got as much weight in flies as meat. Elsie had gone home and was very happy and since the family regarded her as an adopted daughter we were feeling left out. Besides the French didn't like us and they were always surly to us.

Dad was always traveling anyway. Dad spent most of his time in the Mediterranean Countries. Off dad went looking for the Holy Grail as far as housing was concerned. I guess he found a housing officer who knew where the vacancies were. There was housing in the town of Friedberg which is a couple of miles away from Bad Neuheim. There was an American barracks there and a school. The house was a good middle class house. There was only one little problem with the area, which we choose to overlook. We were a few miles, twenty or so, from the Russian occupied sector. Probably could get along with the Russians much better than the French anyway.

Christmas was coming and we needed a nest for the season. Besides, Christmas in Germany meant Advent Calendars, Marzipan, edible Ginger Bread Houses and snow. Not something a ten year old wants to miss. Let's load up the Morris Minor and get going. I do remember dad promising mom that after we got back to Germany he would buy a bigger car.

While we were driving towards Friedberg we went to visit some family friends in Augsburg. They recommended the restaurant in the Hotel in Bad Neuheim. Short story about the friends. They had a Doberman Pincher to protect their property. That dog used to bite everybody who walked into the house including his owners. They got burgled one night when they weren't home. Not only did the burglar and the dog get along, they raided the refrigerator and must have enjoyed the food because they emptied it. We stopped at the hotel in Bad Neuheim for dinner. The restaurant was first class with a large aquarium to the right of the dining room entrance doorway. In the tank were various species of edible fish and ells. Their menu also contained deep fried jumbo prawns, a dozen to a plate. I think the first time I had rice with the prawns. After that I switched from rice to french fries. That lasted on any given Saturday evening until we moved from Friedberg. The waiters all knew me and as soon as we walked through the front door of the hotel, my prawns would be cooking. I guess I was kind of a joke there, but those prawns were delicious.

After we moved into the house the American barracks gave us a start. It was evening; we had finished dinner and were reading until it was time to go to bed. Dad was in Greece or Turkey, or somewhere like that. All of a sudden an air raid siren started to blast. We couldn't tell where it was coming from, but our thoughts were on the soviets a few miles away. I went outside to the front of the house to catch the first sight of the Russian bombers coming over. The streets were dark, all of the street lights were off and no lights were on in the houses along our block. I stayed on our block not wanting to get trapped during the bombing. I waited outside for a long time and finally went back into the house when mom told me that there had been an announcement on the radio that it was only a fire in one the barracks and the fire engines had not changed their sirens. In Europe the European standard for air raids is the normal rising and falling mechanical siren of US fire engines, circa 1950, and the European fire engine siren is like you hear in European or English movies, kind of like bells.

My big Christmas present for the year was a pellet rifle. Ya know, living six thousand miles from home and having your normal youth disrupted seems to be working out great for me. I wonder what things are going to be like when we go home?

I went hiking in a forest area not far from the house. As I was walking through the trees I sighted something that was red, you know kind of like a paint red. I went over to investigate and found the Nazi traffic sign complete with the swastika and eagle on it. In pre-war Germany traffic cops directed the traffic; traffic lights were not available and traffic cops had been used since the invention of the motorcar making the traffic cop a part of the culture. In Germany at that time if you wanted to be a cop you had to be a member of the Nazi Party. The cop who was issued the sign was probably more than anxious to get rid of it.

I think mom was getting desperate with dad in the Mediterranean and us in Germany. There was some talk of moving to Naples since it had housing available and an American school plus the amities that would be available through the Navy's Sixth Fleet. I think life was very problematic for mom and damaging mom and dad's marriage. I don't think that NATO is very happy either since Turkey and Greece are causing problems; the culture is so different from the western Europeans. Political graft also permeated those countries after the war. All of these things are delaying the inclusion of those countries into NATO and dad was right in the middle with his budgets. Add the problems of the separated family and dad must have been feeling a great deal of pressure.

So dad finds a place to live in Naples. I have to describe the apartment because it is unusual. Imagine a box; the size doesn't make any difference. From the top/left corner of the box go down about one third from the top/left corner. That's the street driveway. The top line is a masonry retaining wall containing the upper terrace and is about a hundred feet high. The wall on the right contains the apartment's garages. The bottom line is the outside wall of the apartments. We'll call this ground level. On the balance of the left line is a basement apartment with a huge picture window looking into the apartment's living room. Inside the window is a full size concert grand piano. The roof of the garages is the floor of our garden. There are citrus trees and miscellaneous plants planted in our garden. Our apartment is nothing great but it's acceptable.

Back to the trip. We're going to Naples; the trip will be made in the Hillman Minx. Dad bought the Hillman Minx when we got to Friedberg. Everything is loaded up and off we go. We are going through the Dolomites onto the Italian "boot". The Dolomites are steep and full of switchbacks. Dad must have met a race car driver somewhere because he is showing me how a race car driver would negotiate turns like these switchbacks. You can tell mom doesn't appreciate the way dad is driving because of the tone of her voice. We finally get to the bottom of the mountains onto the Italian plane. Italy is neither lush nor impressive. It's dry and looks like it could use some real rain. It's the same country as the scenery in the spaghetti westerns. It gets better when we get close to Rome. We can see Venice in the distance as we are passing on the highway, but we bypass it. It was a very unimpressive ride. We finally got to Naples.

The common saying at that time was "See Naples and Die". The pilots flying over Naples had another saying "You can smell it at twenty thousand feet". It did have a significant aroma. When we got there we went to a hotel/restaurant that was frequented by Errol Flynn. We didn't get to see him; I really wanted his autograph because I loved his pirate movies. Evidentially you had to get to the hotel early because he would drink himself into a stupor and the hotel staff would take him to his room.

There was another restaurant in Naples that was known for its good food and some of the customers. I don't remember the name of the restaurant but it was known for being the favorite restaurant of the "Italian boy who went to America and made good". That guys name was Lucky Luciano.

We moved into the apartment without too much fuss. We weren't the only Americans in the complex. There was a Navy

Lieutenant Commander and his wife living across the hall. You've got to remember these people because they add to the story later. The garden came in handy; I could get my pellet rifle out and target practice.

I started school and we settled into a normal life. We have scenic elements well within sight. The most famous is Vesuvius. The smoke and steam are coming from its mantle, but you don't see any lava flows or anything. I had never seen a volcano before so I was interested. I heard about Pompeii so I wanted to go there before we left. It seems that if you wanted to see any of the sights in an area you had to get with it. As a family, we had no long range plans.

Our neighborhood was kind of weird. Everything was on terraces going up a hill. There were retaining walls on the backsides of each terrace. Each of the retaining walls extended above the roadway leaving a guard rail with a bench where people could sit. Now my mom was Victorian modest. One day she noticed a woman clothed in black garb breast feeding an infant and sitting on the retaining wall bench directly across from our apartment. She gave the maid a few hundred lire with the instructions for the woman to move on. The next morning, bright and early, there were six women dressed in black garb sitting on that wall and breast feeding infants. They looked like a flight of blackbirds sitting on a telephone line. After that day the Catholic Clergy in Naples decided that our apartment was the Treasury of the Vatican. Sometimes you had to wait in line to get into the damn apartment. The priests and nuns finally got tired of hearing "no" and stopped begging.

My own personal problems were simple in comparison. I was going to school in an American school that had more

THE CAMP FOLLOWER

bomb scares than fire drills, and got tired of chasing the Italian kids after they spit in my face on the way home from school. The neat thing is that I had become friends with the apartment building concierge and his wife. Both parents plus all of their kids were obese, and they had a bunch of kids. There was a good reason for their obesity, the wife made her own pasta and raviolis and spaghetti and other delicious food. And they would invite me down to their apartment for dinner. I think my folks were jealous. I did get to bring food back to our apartment. I don't think these people felt comfortable around my folks, I'm not sure why.

Let's get back to the basement apartment. The guy who lived there was either an opera star or a wannabe. He would entertain a couple of times a week. His regimen consisted of having a siesta from two to four and than start preparing dinner. Dinner was eaten between ten and twelve with singing starting at midnight. There were solos and choruses and everyone in the apartment complex could hear it.

I came down with Pneumonia but couldn't go to the Navy Hospital because there were no beds available. The American sailors were suffering through some kind of an epidemic, filling the hospital. The Navy doctor had to make house calls to the apartment and fill me up with antibiotics. I was one sick puppy; I couldn't even lift my head off the pillow and needed help to go to the bathroom. One day I had a visit from an Italian policeman with a translator. He wanted to know if I had shot the basement opera signer with my pellet rifle at about one o'clock in the morning. Of course I said no. He wanted to see my rifle, so mom got it for him out of my closet. He was convinced when he compared the calibers from the pellet shot at the opera singer and the caliber of my rifle. I noticed a very strange look on mom's face for just a second during the questioning, like she was asking herself if I did it. I was off the hook. Turns out that the Lieutenant Commander shot the singer and hit him in the head or neck or something. The singer was not seriously hurt, but he had to stop singing, the picture window had a nice round hole in it from the pellet and everybody in the apartment building got a good nights sleep. Dad became very angry at the Lieutenant Commander for not having the honesty to admit that he had shot the singer; and that he had let a kid take the fall for what he had done. Dad didn't disapprove of the shooting itself. But wait, there's more. We haven't gotten to this guys wife.

The next few months were uneventful with the family going out on tourist excursions. The Italians had given the Navy a beach for the exclusive use of the Navy personnel, of course we were included. Turns out that the beach was next to an open sewer line. It kind of makes you feel funny when you're swimming along and notice turds bobbing in the surf. The beach was lousy too. It was made up of pebbles instead of sand and the pebbles were large enough to make walking difficult.

We went to Pompeii and wandered around the town in all the places that were open to the public. It was interesting to see the dead bodies that had been covered with ash in their own form and preserved for a couple of thousand years. Some of the excavations were fresh, so we were seeing parts of the town that hadn't been seen in two thousand years. Now that's exciting. I got an appreciation for the technology that the ancient Romans used in construction and infrastructure. There was running water and concrete and communal toilets and baths. Of course I couldn't see myself using the toilets with a whole bunch of other people. I guess that I had more Irish in me than I thought.

We went to Capri and saw all of the beautiful gardens, which I had no interest in. I put the hotel in the same category and I think there was a palace there. The only thing that caught my attention was the boat ride into the blue grotto. Not so much for the water seeming to be blue, but the boat ride itself. We went on a trip to Salerno; quite frankly I don't even remember that trip.

The most interesting trip, at least from my perspective, was a trip to some dormant volcanoes. These were volcanoes that had formed caps at the top of their mantles and these caps were thick enough to hold a car and people. We drove out onto one of them, got out of the car and our guide jumped up and down on the cap to prove that there was nothing beneath the cap because it sounded hollow. That was fun. Mom had been warned before we started this trip that Sulfur and Sulfur compounds would dissolve certain artificial clothing materials like Rayon. Mom was wearing a Rayon dress, I remember the dress. It was a light green print with flower leaves on it. I watched it slowly dissolve until she retreated to the car. There were hotspots all over the caldera. There were a few with geothermal springs. The areas that grabbed my attention were a couple of hotspots where there was boiling gravel and sand. You could certainly tell they were hot because you could feel the heat from a couple of feet away and they would bubble like boiling water. That was the most interesting attraction, at least to my point of view. I have always had an affinity for nature, simply can't get enough of it.

Dad had some leave coming up and the Sixth Fleet was planning a cruise through the Mediterranean as a show of presence. Dad arranged our passage on one of the Fleets ships equipped for passengers. We were going to travel to Greece and Turkey. Dad was in Greece at the time so that made our vacation possible. The Lieutenant Commander's wife wanted to go along, her husband was assigned to one of the other ships, and they wanted to make a vacation of it. We would meet dad in Athens and go from there. I think dad joined us on the voyage from Athens to Istanbul.

It was lunch time on the second day out at sea and the Lieutenant Commander's wife wanted to join us for lunch. Mom told me to go down to her stateroom and see if she was ready for lunch. I went down to her stateroom and knocked on the door. She opened the door giving you the impression she was anxiously waiting for someone. I am standing in the doorway looking directly at her naked boobs. It took me a couple of microseconds to realize that she was nude. It took her a little longer to realize it was me. Anyway she closed the door with a bang. A couple of seconds later I heard her in a very plaintive voice say "Johnny, don't say anything about this to your mother". Oh, I agreed, why would I want to tell my mother something like this which would in turn cut off all opportunities for it to happen again. Hell, I just passed my second manhood test.

We went to see the usual tourist attractions. I was getting tired of seeing ruins. The attractions became less important the further we got away from the Acropolis. My interest peaked when we went to the Istanbul Bazaar. Most things were made of brass and shinny. I really wanted a scimitar sword, but the folks said no. With that sword, when we got back to Naples I would have gone screaming down the street chasing those Italian kids who spit in my face with my sword in my hand. After all, I had already been accused of shooting a guy who kept the neighborhood up all night why not de-capatate some Italian kid? We cruised back to Naples. It was a fun trip, and even learned something about a woman's anatomy.

A few weeks later we got an emergency message that dad was in a Turkish hospital with bleeding ulcers. He had been in there for a couple of days and was not doing well. The Turks and Greeks had culturally and physiologically beaten him. We travelled to Istanbul to see him; meanwhile the army was arranging for his transport. He walked out of that hospital, and we went back to Naples. As soon as he could he requested a transfer on humanitarian grounds and the army found an open position in the finance office in Munich.

We're getting ready for our fifth move in less than three years in three separate countries. I am eleven years old and have seen more of the world than most of my peer group, and the majority of American adults. This condition has been so prevalent I may have trouble readjusting to a normal life.

Off we go in the Hillman Minx to Munich. The trip is uneventful. Dad has some leave coming so we traveled to Rome and then on to Florence and stayed for a couple of days in each place. In Rome we went to see all of the sights including the Vatican. The Coliseum was pretty impressive because of its size and construction. In Florence we went through all of the historical places and bought leather items and wallets. The leather is beautiful but it's not pracatible. From there we drove to Mezzegra where Mussolini and his mistress were executed and then on to Milan to see the gas station where Mussolini was hung by his heels. Then it was off to mom's favorite drive; the Dolomites, into Bavaria, and finally to Munich.

Dad's new assignment is a regular office job so we really lived as a normal family. The house we were assigned was pretty nice, even a room for a live-in housekeeper. Munich has a well established army base with all the American amenities. It was pretty popular as an assignment since it had a historical Hof Brau Haus. There was Little League Baseball, Boy Scouts and all the other American amenities, just like in the U.S. To me it is too Americanized which in my mind is boring considering the last two years have been very interesting. We will be able to see the local sights, go on weekend trips and just play tourist; and see Europe. We can't go to any country behind the Iron Curtain, but we can go to the countries jointly administrated by the Allies.

I joined the Little League and was welcomed because of my size. I played Center Field and only stayed on the team because I could hit the ball a mile. My modus operandi was that I would swing and miss twice, or hit a foul ball, and then hit the ball for at least a base hit. This was not intentional but it did surprise me, as well as the other team. I got bored with Little League and didn't go to practice for a week. When I went back I found out that I had been chosen for the All Star Game but nobody told me so I didn't go.

I don't remember joining a Boy Scout troop, so I guess I didn't. I don't know why. I guess I was used to not having American things to do; it would take me awhile to re-adjust to American life.

THE CAMP FOLLOWER

Our first trip is to Vienna. We spent the weekend there and saw the museums, the house that Mozart lived in and the historical monuments. We wandered into the Russian sector of the city where there was a statue, of who I don't remember, but it did have a couple of Russian sentries marching around the statue in the classical goosestep march. This is the same marching step that the American propaganda machine ridiculed the Germans for during the war and as it turns out is used all around the world. I wanted to take a picture of the Russians, but dad said no. As we were leaving Vienna I saw the biggest Ferris wheel in the world. Didn't get to ride it but it was impressive. It had been used as a prop in the movie "The Third Man" starring Orson Welles. I even remember the movie and seeing Orson Welles standing in front of the Ferris wheel using a telephone.

Our next weekend trip was to the town of Berchtesgaden. The town was a favorite of the Nazis and in 1953 stood as it had at the end of the war. We stayed at the Berchtesgadener Hof hotel which I understand was kind of Nazi central. The hotel was very nice and the hotel's restaurant was historically amazing. The hotel had most of the linen napkins embroidered with the swastika and eagle on them. The silverware also had the swastika cast into each piece. Dad decided that it was a good opportunity to steal a couple of napkins and pieces of silverware in spite of the Military Police guarding the restaurant. He got caught with the silverware and had to put it back. He did get away with the napkins, I've wondered for years what happened to them. Someone must have stolen them from us.

The Alps always intrigued me, they were so majestic. We took a trip to the Eagles Nest. It was very interesting and not like the mini-series it has been depicted in, the main room was huge with a huge glass window looking out to the terrace and then overlooking the valley. It was kind of a mess when we got there with rubble all over the floor in the main room. I can't remember if the rest of the rooms were open, seems like we didn't go much farther than the main room. I say the main room as in living room.

We went to Saltsburg and then on to the Konigsee to take a boat tour of the lake. The lake is beautiful and kind of weird. It's surrounded by shear cliffs and is probably the best lake in the world for echoes. The water is very clear and looks like you could pick up a glass of water from the lake and drink it. It has an island housing the St. Bartholomä and Watzmann church.

The folks were in a great discussion if we should go on the tour of Dachau because of its history. They decided to put that trip off until they believed it would not adversely affect me. Our time was running out for the weekend and we wanted to get home, besides we could make Dachau a day trip. It's not far from Munich. The folks decide that Dachau will not be too devastating on me; we'll make it a day trip. We have no idea what we are going to see or how we will feel when we get there. We know that this is one of hundreds of camps operated by the Nazi's, and we know that thousands of people were murdered there and it was one of the smaller camps. I couldn't understand then or now how a society could do something like this. I never believed that the general population didn't know about this, it was announced in the newspapers. We get to the camp and the first thing we are shown are the barracks with the explanation that when the camp was in operation

Dachau Creamatorium Oven

with political prisoners and anyone else the Nazi's wanted to get rid of there were at least five times the number of people occupying each barrack as it was designed to hold.

Next we go to the gas chambers. As we are walking into the chamber I get this uneasy feeling of the unknown and then sheer terror while we are in there, even though I know that nothing is going to happen to me. The gas chamber is simply a large room with nothing inside. The ceiling houses shower heads and ventilators. The floor has floor drains to wash the excrement off the floor after the gassing. The last moments of those poor people's lives must have been insurmountable terror. Just standing there you get the feeling that there are hundreds of thousands of ghosts screaming for help. Next we see the Crematoriums, which are housed on one side of a shed. There must have been twenty ovens in that room. I can't understand; even today how a sophisticated and gentle people who gave us Beethoven and Mozart could do such things. You can't blame the Germans without blaming the Russians, Americans on both continents, Cambodians, and all the modern countries who practice ethnic cleansing. Maybe it is the true human condition to do something so abhorrent with impunity. It simply made me want to analyze my belief in god and religion.

It was time to go skiing in Garmish. We went down there for a week and I really enjoyed it. The only thing they have for a lift on the bunny hill is a rope tow. I screw up more on the rope tow then skiing down the hill. The damn thing stops all the time and of course I don't, or I start going sideways or backwards and fall, with the people behind me crashing into me. You have to remember that they are just as experienced as I am. Never did perfect my rope tow expertise; and I never progressed to the next plateau in skiing, in other words past the bunny hill. I took lessons every morning we were there, but to no avail. Actually dad wasn't doing much better than me, but at least he could navigate the hill from top to bottom without falling. I felt so clumsy because I couldn't learn to ski well. I would have given it up except that Christmas my big gift was skis, boots and poles. A half a block down the street from the house was an empty lot with a huge mound of dirt on it. After a good snow, I used to go down there and practice going down that hill. Unfortunately we were going home and I never really got good at it. Our tour in Europe was coming to an end. I started wondering what it would be like living in the States again.

Dad has been re-assigned to the Army Audit Agency in Chicago. He will be the regional chief for the Midwest Region. For one horrible moment I thought dad was going to ship the Hillman Minx to the states. In the end he ordered a 1953 Chevy Bel Air for delivery in New York. I don't remember the name of the ship we came back on; I guess because sailing the Atlantic was second nature to me now. The trip was the reverse of the trip going to Germany. There were a couple of exceptions; one of the kid's father had a Zenith Transoceanic radio which the kid got to use, and we were travelling during hurricane season. The trip was uneventful until we were two days out of New York. We were skirting a tropical storm or hurricane, I really don't know which. We took the Zenith radio to the roof of the bridge to see if we could pick up a New York radio station. Well, we did pick up a New York broadcast station and all of a sudden the program broke for a commercial with a jingle. It was a toothpaste commercial, I remember something about whiter teeth. AFN doesn't broadcast any commercials and absolutely doesn't broadcast jingles. I thought that the jingle was the stupidest thing I had ever heard and told everyone who would listen that I thought so. We disembarked and went to Governors Island, the new car was waiting for us in Manhattan. We were home in the US again. If mom cried when we passed the Statute of Liberty on our way to Germany, you should have seen the buckets she cried when we passed on our way to the dock. To me it was just the continuation of an adventure. We were going to stay at the BOQ on Governors Island the first night and then move to a hotel in Manhattan for the rest of our stay in New York.

We checked into the BOQ and the folks wanted a drink before dinner at the Officers Club. I was allowed into the bar with them even through I was twelve years old. Above the bar attached to the wall there was a one eyed monster called a TV like I saw in Heidelberg more than three years before. Howdy Doody was playing on the TV. I wasn't so much interested in Howdy Doody as much as the picture itself. I'm standing there with my mouth open staring. The next day we move to the hotel in Manhattan. Dad decides that we can spend a couple of days here before taking off for Chicago. The first order of business for dad was to pick up the car from the dealer. While he was doing that mom and I, and some friends from the boat decided to do a little sightseeing. I was so enthralled with the tall buildings I stumbled into wet cement on the sidewalk. The tradesmen who were installing the cement were not enthralled with me. I apologized and got my ass out of there. We went to Grand Central Station and the top of the Empire State Building, as well as other places including department stores. All in all it was a fantastic sightseeing tour.

THE CAMP FOLLOWER

Off we went to Chicago. We got onto the Turnpike and headed west. The only things that made the trip even mildly interesting were the toll booths. I don't even remember a Burma Shave sign. As we got closer to some town, don't know which, there was a sign advertising something and mom pointed it out to me. My only reply was that I couldn't read the sign. You could almost see the light bulbs going on above my folk's heads as they were looking at each other in disbelief. Their son had poor eyesight. After all the "I didn't know, I was asked what I thought about eyeglasses. They explained that if I had eyeglasses I would be able to see much better. The writing on that sign wasn't that small. Anyway I made an unconscious decision to put off the dyslexia admission until another occasion.

We rented a house in Glenview which is a suburb of Chicago. The only thing that happened while we were there that was exciting was that dad bought a TV. I'm back in civilian life again and I don't like it. Either the army or dad or somebody decided to move the audit agency office to Kansas City. Dad went to Kansas City found some office space, went back to Glenview and the office in Chicago, made arrangements to move the office and its personnel, got mom, went back to Kansas City and they bought a house. Off we go to Kansas City. The house is nicer than the one in Glenview. I'm OK with the house because I am in an attic space that had been converted to a bedroom and was very comfortable. The walls and ceiling were knotty pine and I even have good sized dormer window that allows me to get out on the roof.

The neat thing about Kansas City is that it was compact. We live on the Kansas side of the city. We can go to the

Kansas City Stockyards and have a good prime rib or steak fairly easily. That wasn't true in Chicago, fighting traffic to the stockyards and through the city. To me the neatest thing was the "Starlight Theater" which was an open air theater and in the summer would show excellent first run Broadway plays with the original New York casts. We saw Oklahoma and Carousel in the same summer. The Starlight also provided relief from the oppressive heat. It was 1954 and air conditioning was not common. I was in the eighth grade of a parochial school and had my first opportunity to play football. That was also my first and last experience as an alter boy. I was drafted to do both. My size made me a football candidate and the fact that I was the only boy in the eighth grade who hadn't become an alter boy made me a target for a young priest.

The priest organized the effort to make me look like an alter boy. It was decided that for the alter boys response to the priests prayers I would mumble. Hell, I didn't know any Latin. Since the alter boy with the bell didn't move around the alter much, I was given the bell. The regular alter boy would give me hand signals when I was supposed to ring the bell. That plan can't go wrong; you wanna bet? Everything was going according to plan and even mom came to the early weekday mass to see her son perform as an alter boy. The other guy gives me the signal; I pick up the bell and start to ring it. For some reason the clapper in the bell refused to go from side to side enabling it to go ding-dong; but instead spun inside the bell housing going Rrrrrrrrrrrrrrrr, I can't make it stop, the priest is giving me dirty looks because he thinks that I am doing it on purpose. I'm going to Hell just as soon as this mass is over. Nobody in the church is laughing, although most of the attendees are elderly citizens, probably can't hear well. I am embarrassed to think I can't even ring a bell correctly. I think my alter boy career is over!

Football was more fun. The only thing I didn't like about the football team was that my favorite priest, yep that one, was the coach. I can tell he doesn't like me that much either. I tried to tell him on several occasions that the bell incident was not planned by me or anyone else. Personally I think it was just God's way to telling us that not all boys should be alter boys. I liked to play basketball too. Once when a group of us were playing in the playground after school I jumped for a layup, made the basket, and collided with the pipe standard for the basket. Now my aim couldn't have been better. I hit the pipe with my mouth and broke one front tooth and chipped the other.

Dad is on the promotion list for promotion to Full Colonel. He had come back from the Second World War as a Lieutenant Colonel and was getting anxious about any further promotions. He is all excited about the promotion and it finally comes through. We are all so proud of him.

The next door neighbor was a captain on what I remember as United Airlines. He had a charter from New York to Kansas City with the entire musical complement of "Jazz at the Philharmonic". He was such a nice guy and always so good to me that he found a concert program and had all of the headliners autograph it. Since I was a jazz aficionado I loved it. I often wonder what happened to it; it disappeared from my folk's garage. That family had more than enough problems; their last child who was a baby when we lived there was born with a hole in her heart. She lived for a few years and then her affliction overcame her and she died. Her parents were always supportive and loving. I know that mom always held Marge, the mother, in the highest esteem for providing the love and care for her child.

The last story I can remember from Kansas City was a baseball game. Dad invited me to a baseball game between the Kansas City Athletics and the New York Yankees. I couldn't say no because Mickey Mantle was playing. He was my hero. Dad got seats in center field about five rows up in the bleachers. That was just in case that Mickey Mantle hit one out of center field into the bleachers and into my hands. It didn't happen but I was happy just the same. I'm probably one of the last surviving fans of the Kansas City Athletics since they have been playing in Oakland California for so long. I thought the ballpark was fun. It was in a residential neighborhood with houses bordering one side of the park. The roofs of the houses were full of people watching the game for free.

It was October 1954 and the new car models had hit the showrooms. The unveiling of the new models resulted in the showrooms being very busy during the first couple of months of the new model year. Dad was of the opinion that you should trade in your car every two years. That was the normal turnover rate if you could afford it. He traded in the 53 Chevy for a 55 Chevy which we'll talk about later. A new car cost about two thousand dollars at that time. That didn't mean you didn't have to make payments, it just gives you the value of a dollar. The idea that American men would look forward to visiting a new car showroom in October to see the unveiling of the new model year has always impressed me. We did it every year until the 60's while we were in the States, whether we could afford the car or not. It just shows how much our society and economy have changed during the years since the Second World War. I wonder if that feeling of having the opportunity of something new, like a new car, on a regular basis is lacking in our present environment.

Dad is being transferred to Fort Bragg North Carolina. We would drive down there in our new Chevy.

18TH AIRBORNE CORPS

Dad was assigned as the Comptroller of the Eighteenth Airborne Corps. It is based in Fort Bragg North Carolina and consisted of the 82nd Airborne Division, the 101st Airborne Division and the then 77th Special Forces "The Green Berets". As I remember the 101st was based at Fort Benning Georgia. The Air Force had a base adjacent to Fort Bragg, Pope Air Force Base. Guess it would be hard to have paratroopers without airplanes. It was kind of neat to be back in a military facility; although I was comfortable in Kansas City.

We moved into our quarters which were very comfortable. It was a well thought out design. In the area we lived the two sides of the streets were separated by a green area with large trees. The green area made the houses look like they all faced on a park.

I think dad felt under the gun to a degree, here he was in a unit almost exclusively paratroopers and he wasn't qualified to jump. Even though he was forty years old and a Full Colonel, and would have to go through rigorous training, he decided that he wanted those jump wings. There was jump pay available for those who were qualified and the extra pay would come in handy. He was even following in the paratrooper footsteps of

THE CAMP FOLLOWER

General Matthew Ridgeway who was given command of the 82nd Airborne before he was qualified as a paratrooper. So dad applied for jump school and got accepted. Off he went to jump school into the arms of the drill instructors who were all sergeants. The first week was pretty rough on him He probably did more pushups in a day than he had done for the rest of his life. He would get home after training and without changing out of his uniform go into the sun porch, lay on the floor in front of the television and go to sleep until it was time to take a shower before dinner. One of his favorite sayings at that time was emulating the drill sergeant with "Colonel give me ten" or fifty or whatever, depending on the Drill Instructors mood. Even if he wanted to he couldn't quit. In jump school there is practice equipment to teach the student how to land without breaking anything. The equipment consists of two sizes of wooden towers at about twenty and thirty feet high. The student is equipped with a regular parachute harness and when he jumps from the tower, he slides down an incline set of cables to a built-up earth berm. As I remember the thirty foot tower emulates the speed you reach on a real jump. Dad had completed all of his training with the exception of the last jump from the thirty foot tower. He was scheduled to make his first jump from a plane the next morning. He left the tower, down the cables hit the berm and broke his ankle. A regular soldier would either have been washed out, quit, or if he was really gung-ho start all over again. Not dad, he was expected to start the training all over again, even if it was for the benefit of is own ego. So now he would work at his office during the day; come home, back to the sun porch, lay on the floor because his cast made it uncomfortable to sit in one of the chairs we had in that room, and watch television until dinner. That went on for six weeks. He went through jump school the second time and got his wings, we were all very proud of him. After graduation the class is expected to have a party to celebrate the graduation. In other words they are all supposed to get drunk. Now dad was a social drinker, two Scotches every night. He was expected to lead the enlisted men in their effort to get drunk at the party. After all he was the Colonel, first out of the plane, first to get drunk. I came home after the graduation party had obviously ended and there was dad sitting on the front steps of the house holding his head in his hands, as sick as a dog. He obviously didn't want anyone to see him so sick.

It was decided that we needed a second car for dad to drive into town when he needed to and he found the perfect car. It was a 1947 Buick convertible. I learned to drive in that car and used to love having the top down.

As for me I was going to junior high school in Fayetteville which is the closest town to Fort Bragg. Fayetteville was a typical southern town of the time, completely segregated with its orange and white sections of everything. Of course when you got back to Fort Bragg, the segregation was informal, but still there. The services were formally integrated in 1947 by Harry Truman but informally there was still segregation. Being rebellious I would sit in the orange side of the bus stop and watch the whities go by, showing their best hate looks. A couple of times while I was sitting on the orange side of the bus stop; I would be conned by a carload of black soldiers. I'm sure that they assumed that I was a local who didn't know any better or had arrived at Fort Bragg that day or mentally deranged and they could take advantage of me pretty easily. They would charge me cab fare equal to the cab fare they would have paid if they had taken a cab. I'm not sure that cab fares back to Fort

**Jump School Graduation
Dad with the classes Drill Instructors**

Bragg were not on a sliding scale depending upon race. So I had to pay for what I thought was the right thing to do in our society, and that was to truly integrate it.

I was fourteen and eligible to join the Explorer Scouts. There was a troop of Air Explorers on the base, and because of my love of airplanes decided to join. The troop had a shack as a meeting hall. As I approached the shack I noticed a group of guys repelling off the roof of the shack and decided that this was for me. I joined immediately. The adult advisor was a drill instructor from the 77th Special Forces. This is going to be more interesting than a civilian troop because of the advisor's experience in the Green Berets. The other parents that were involved in the troop were Air Force pilots and from other specialties at the post. In an environment like that, merit badges became secondary and flying and survival training became the primary interest for me.

Fort Bragg is huge; there were lakes, forests, landing zones, artillery ranges, rifle ranges and the list just goes on. That's where I saw the demonstration of the atomic cannon. What a boondoggle that was; much ado about nothing, the personnel demonstrating the cannon had us using ear plugs, opening our mouths to avoid the concussion and standing way back. In truth the cannon barrel was so long you could barely hear the thing when it was fired. I believe that the cannon faded into obscurity because it had no practical purpose along with the fact that the armed services had perfected missiles. I think that the length of the barrel had something to do with keeping the crew far enough from the target site to minimize the exposure of the crew from radioactive material.

THE CAMP FOLLOWER

There were three golf courses on Fort Bragg. There was the noncommissioned officers golf club, the officers club and a small nine hole course that had been mostly ignored for years. Dad was the President of the Officers Club Golf Club and he decided two very important things. First the club needed a good driving range and second I needed a job for the summer. All of a sudden I was the manager of the driving range, whether I liked it or not. I would have preferred to spend the summer practicing my survival skills and camping and fishing. We took over the abandoned nine hole course and equipped it with distance signs, tee markers, a small shack, lots of brand new range balls and a large Coca Cola cooler. The most sophisticated piece of equipment was the ball pick up. It was a Coca Cola can with the top cut out and a golf club shaft attached for a total capacity of two balls. If I had a crowd, it would have taken most of the day to pick up all of the balls. Luckily I never had a crowd. You have got to figure that the Coke can could hold two golf balls and a bucket of balls contained twenty-five or thirty balls, none of which were in the same place. Dad was serious about teaching me how to run a business. I couldn't care less. He decided to lend me the money to stock the cooler. My little business would have commissary privileges as long as I bought from dad. Nothing wrong with that, the only people who were authorized to use the driving range were military personnel. The cost of selling the drinks was a simple pass-through. We had to decide what to buy for the cooler. It was a foregone conclusion that the cooler would contain Coke, Pepsi, and 7up. Because we were in the south we also stocked it with Grape Soda and Dr Pepper. The question of beer came up and dad was the unanimous vote of one picking his favorite beer, he was the only one to vote.

It was pretty hot at Fort Bragg in the summer. The driving range shack didn't have any cross ventilation and I would have to stand there all day, so to cool down I would drink some of the soft drinks. I picked the Grape Soda because its sales were not too good. I must have had three or four bottles of the soda before closing up. Got home, went through the hell of counting the day's receipts with the help of my father and then had dinner. Went to bed that night and all of a sudden felt a little queasy. I knew I was going to vomit pretty quickly, got out of bed and headed for the bathroom. The bedrooms and a bathroom in the house were on the second floor; and from my bedroom door to the bathroom door was about twenty-five feet. I headed for the bathroom, got halfway down the hall and realized that the bathroom door was closed. I didn't know if someone was in the bathroom or the door was just closed. Didn't make any difference since I shot my Grape Soda torpedo directly at the door and made a perfect shot. Dad's first response was the usual, "What the hell have you done this time?" Mom was a hell of a lot more sympathetic. If you haven't smelled used Grape Soda, you have missed a treat. Anyway I offered to clean up the mess and mom insisted she would do it for me, and I should go back to bed. I hate to admit it but after that experience I would only drink the beer in the cooler and make up stories about where it went, at least that's the excuse I used for myself. At the very least I had to pay for the beer and a few buckets of balls to prove that there were customers that day even if there weren't. I made so little money at that job; most of my wages went for beer and imaginary buckets of balls. That experiment finally came to a close to the whole family's relief. The driving range didn't attract many customers and it was hell to count the day's receipts at the dining room table after dinner with dad's help. Looking back on it, I was counting a lot of pennies and that doesn't make any sense. I didn't use pennies in the operation.

The junior high school in Fayetteville was not what I was used to. First it was a segregated school and the rumor was that the black school was scholastically better than ours. The same rumor also included the high school, it was said that there were more graduates from the black high school who went on to a military academy than our white school. Our school was more like a trade school. I remember the wood shop teacher didn't have all his fingers, but I can say that I only saw one student cut off one of his fingers while I was there. I got into trouble with my Spanish teacher, she couldn't speak Spanish. Being from California I knew how to pronounce the names of the cities in the Bay Area correctly. She insisted in pronouncing the name San Jose with the English pronunciation of the letter J so she would pronounce it San JO-se. I kept trying to get her to accept the fact that in Spanish you pronounce a J as an H, and the correct pronunciation is San Hosay. She never caught on or if she was corrected by someone who knew, didn't want to back down.

Mike was my best friend, we were inseparable. We went hiking and camping through the rest of the summer and had a great deal of fun whatever we did. Mike's father was one of the Protestant Chaplains on the base. Mike's dad was very close to Mike, they really enjoyed fishing together. Mike and I went camping together all the time, once we had my mother drop us off because we were going to a remote spot. I guess that I should explain that this was the days before camping became a family affair with all the modern conveniences. We had World War Two surplus army issue shelter half's for tents, army mummy bags for sleeping bags and a pump up kerosene stove right out of a soldier's backpack, I think it was dads. Good thing that dad never had to go on bivouac because he no longer had a stove and was responsible for it; and you can imagine how much pleasure it would give some Quartermaster lieutenant to make out that form. My diet on these camping trips was quite simple, steamed onions. Couldn't get the hang of boiling potatoes on that stove, they never got cooked, or they took so long to cook that I had already eaten the onions and wasn't hungry anymore and threw the potatoes out. From my perspective meat was out of the question. Anyway, we set up camp about a half a mile away from a building; I think it was a soldiers club. There were sentries on duty at this building, probably trainees from the Green Berets. It started to rain furiously, so we climbed into the tent and just had a good time. Now you have to realize that the army didn't care if its soldiers got wet if they were living in these shelter halves' and using mummy bags. That's what we were doing, getting wet. All of a sudden we hear a car horn which is familiar to me, it's our Buick convertible. Inside the car are my folks and they don't want to get out of the car and get wet, that's why they were blowing the horn so that we would have to go to the car and get wetter. We run over to the car, dad lowers the window and tells us that we are driving the sentry's nuts and they have even called their unit for permission to shoot at the intruders, that's us. After the very short discussion we get into the car and are taken home. It is also explained that we could pick up our gear tomorrow. I think dad had a conversation with the sentry's immediate commanding officer regarding where this guy got live ammunition.

The Commanding Officer for the Corps was Major General Paul Adams. There was also another Paul Adams on the base,

THE CAMP FOLLOWER

he was our age and not liked. In fact he had to suffer through everything we could hurl at him in the way of insults and chides. We did not bully him and he had more than a better chance to rebut us. Now this Paul Adams had been invited to a party and we weren't invited. Not that it mattered to us since Air Explorers would not take a back seat to anyone. We are on an airborne post after all. We were walking down the sidewalk at the back of the quarters when we heard the younger Adams talking in a loud voice at the party. There was a hedge between us and the backyard of the quarters so we couldn't see into the backyard. We started our chiding of Paul. In a few minutes I noticed a pair of boots next to me with the pants bloused at the boots indicating a paratrooper. I slowly looked up until I met the eyes of an MP who was asking me who I was and who my father was. I dutifully answered him and asked why he was interested. He carefully informed me that we had been chiding the younger Paul across the street from General Adams quarters and he could hear it. I wondered if dad would make it quick and shoot me or if he would slowly hang me. I probably had until tomorrow afternoon at about five PM to live. The next day I found out that you can get so mad that you can't talk. General Adams had dad on the carpet for a full half hour and he wanted to make sure that I understood exactly how long a half hour is when you can't respond to any of the screaming aimed at you. There was no love lost between the General and dad. In fact before dad and General Adams were transferred to Fort Bragg, and dad was still the regional chief of the Army Audit Agency, General Adams wrote a critique of the audit agency in which he said that the agency was useless and a waste of time and money. That critique was submitted to the Pentagon so you can see how popular he was with dad.

Another thing that irritated the General was that dad had been appointed as the coordinator of the All-Army Pro Amateur Golf Tournament. This took him away from his regular duties as the Comptroller because this tournament was very important to the army. There were notable professional golfers in the tournament that had to be taken care of. To make matters worse the tournament was a complete success and dad got commendations for his efforts from the Pentagon.

The survival training was fun. It was modeled after the real thing with teams set up to compete against each other for the training. We learned how to trap and prepare certain animals for food. We never did kill or hurt any animals during the training. What we did was to take meat from the commissary and use it as wild game. We did eat the vegetation that we found that was recommended by our adult advisor. Everybody's favorite, to talk about anyway, was the opossum since it was so popular in the South and it was said that it was good for breakfast. We learned how to build traps for both animals and man using only our hunting knives and string, or bark. The most important thing we learned is that you can survive in the forest without any modern tools and can be totally self-reliant. To that end we could climb trees, repel down cliffs, and the other things that the Special Forces do, which made us self-sufficient during any emergency.

We were going on a navigation exercise. I was appointed as a squad leader by the adult advisor. The exercise comprised of finding a way around a lake in the middle of the night. I had five or six guys with me. The object of the exercise was first to find our way around the lake; and second to establish a communication link for cooperation between the members of our group. Mike was there and was very supportive. We started at the head of the lake and made our way down the length of the lake. Then to save time I decided to cut across the bottom end of the lake. We wandered into a swamp that just started getting deeper and the foliage got thicker. I remember that the depth of the swamp was up to our waists at its deepest. Mike was still supportive, the rest of the guys wanted to leave by the way we came in. I still thought we could save time by pushing ahead. In either case moving around the forest with a flashlight in the dark of night is an experience. I was worried about snakes and other animals like snapping turtles that lived in the swamp. We finally made it through and less than flushed with success reported to the adult advisor who gave me a very strange look. I don't know if he approved of my plan or not, probably not.

It's pretty hard to take a ride in an Air Force plane if you are a civilian. A gaggle of fourteen year olds make the approval process even more difficult. The only airplanes that were available to us were C-47's, the same plane as the DC-3, left over from the Second World War. These planes were the same model of planes used for the invasion of Europe by the 82nd and 101st airborne into France and Belgium during the D-Day invasion. It's the morning of our first flight and we have assembled in the hanger. We are advised that we must wear parachutes for the flight. The parachute riggers are there to fit the parachutes. Everything was cool until it was time to tighten the harness straps. You have two straps going through your legs in the groin area. Do you know that the parachute rigger can lift a man off the floor by pulling on those straps. We were told that those straps are the most important on the harness since they hold the parachutist in the rigging. Next we had to walk out to the flight line, climb the steps into the plane and get through the door. My respect for the airborne corps is growing immensely during the walk. I can't remember if the seats were forward facing or airborne benches along the side of the aircraft. Anyway we took off and got to ride around for awhile, at best a very bumpy ride. It's hard to imagine sixteen paratroopers packed into a plane with their equipment and going into battle in France or Belgium during the Second World War. I am surprised that any of them made it. Either the airborne personnel are the bravest of the brave or completely nuts. Imagine you are floating down to the earth and a bullet is rushing up to meet you at several hundred feet per second.

It was a couple of weeks after our navigation exercise, Mike and his father had gone on a fishing trip at the same lake where we had the exercise. They were going to use their canoe. The next morning mom took me aside told me to sit down and sat down with me. That was an ominous moment for me, if everything was normal I was going to get hell for something I did and didn't remember. It was very serious, she told me that Mike and his father were missing and the search team had found their car and canoe at the lake. I went into instant denial explaining that Mike knew that area of the forest well and they had probably wandered off to see what they could find. It was a couple of days when either they had recovered the bodies by dragging the lake or the bodies had simply floated to the surface. I missed my friend Mike for several years. Now I don't know why but after I found out about Mike and his father, my thoughts turned to Mike's mother. Of course this was a disaster but it no longer affected Mike or his father. The people it affected were Mike's mother and siblings. I don't care how important you are at your death; your family must make certain arrangements immediately after your death. The first thing in the army is that the army has a waiting list for the place you are living in and you are a dependant without much clout. You got to pack up your household goods and move. Another thing to consider is that Mike's father was eligible to be buried in a National Cemetery, but Mike wasn't. It's hard when you have to meld two different environments instantly.

Dad and I were driving home from where I don't remember and he started a conversation with me regarding the Air Force. He was asking me for advice, which was unbelievable and he was expecting an adult answer. He told me that the Air Force offered him a Brigadiers General's star if he will transfer to the Air Force. He is hesitant because the Air Force was such a young service and didn't have the tradition or the discipline of the Army. My only response is that he should take it because if they are that hard up for generals, it would probably result in thirty years of service before retirement for him. In the final analysis he decided to stick with the Army, which I still think was a mistake.

Dad was re-assigned to Viet Nam. Nobody knew where Viet Name was, so now we are going to a place that we had never heard of before. Now all we have to do is to find a National Geographic magazine with a World Map in it and find Viet Nam. Somebody pointed out that if the map had been published before 1954 it would have been called French Indochina. So here we are, with the French again.

MAAG VIET-NAM

Dad was assigned to the Military Assistance Advisory Group in Saigon Viet Nam. His job was Comptroller, which required close interaction with the Vietnamese government under President Diem. There are only about six hundred army advisors assigned there, both officers and enlisted ranks. The commander was Lieutenant General Samuel Williams. General Williams was an interesting person. During the Second World War he was a Brigadier General. Evidentially he got into a dispute with someone and was demoted to Colonel. Thereafter he rose in rank to Lieutenant General before he retired. I don't know why but his nickname was "Hanging Sam".

Prior to 1954 MAAG was formed to assist the French in keeping the insurgents, the Viet Minh, from taking over the country. The leader of the Viet Minh was a guy named Ho Chi Minh, who was one of our strongest allies during the Second World War, and who had been fighting for Viet Nam's independence from France since he was a teenager.

Viet Nam had been fighting invaders since the first century including the Chinese and the Japanese, as well as the French. The Japanese occupied the country during the Second World War. The French occupied the country as a colony before the war and re-established themselves after the war was over. It's even said that the French government would not let Ho Chi Min into the French Parliament when he wanted to discuss his countries future after the Second World War. Basically he was ignored by the French.

The US assistance was to replace equipment that had been destroyed during the fighting and to supply essential materials including food. The French, wanting to keep the country as a colony would not support the Vietnamese army just in case they turned on the French Army. The French had to stand alone without local support and fight the Viet Minh. Oh, I forgot to mention that the French had exported thousands of tons of rubber from their rubber plantations on a yearly basis. The Viet Minh beat the shit out of the French in 1954. The Viet Minh had so little respect for the French they didn't take any prisoners. The country was partitioned into North and South Viet Nam. The French had to leave by treaty so the US assisted the South Vietnamese government directly.

The Viet Minh became the Viet Cong, so I guess you could say that dad's assignment was coming during an intermission of the war in Viet Nam's history. Like Korea, the likelihood of a partitioned Viet Nam without a war of reunification was slight. As an example of the insurgency the United States Information Service Library was blown up before dad arrived. The library was the propaganda wing of the CIA. There were six Canadian officers stabbed to death while sleeping in a Bachelor Officer Quarters in Saigon. The BOQ was guarded by military and Vietnamese police.

It was suggested that we get left at home for this assignment. Viet Nam was too hot for us to live in because of its political strife.

We drove across the country in the '55 Chevy towing a one wheel trailer. The trailer wasn't meant to be driven fast but dad didn't care. We had to change the tire a couple of times going across the country. That meant the first time, we had the dismount the wheel, go into town, have the tire fixed and take the wheel back to the trailer. If it could happen once it could happen twice, so dad bought a spare wheel and tire. Now someone had to guard the trailer while having the tire repaired, and guess who got that duty, why its mom. I remember seeing her while we were driving back to the trailer and she truly looked dissolute sitting on the corner of the trailer. This lacked all of the romance of our trip in 1950 and we didn't even appreciate the roads Eisenhower had arranged for us. Bottom line, we were in a hurry. We stopped in Dodge City because it was a cattle railhead during the Cowboy's cattle drives from Texas and there was a restaurant that had a sign in the window that said "Real Kansas Beef". We stopped there for dinner and had an exciting meal. I'm not exaggerating when I say that I have boots with a thicker soles than the steak we were served. Not only was it thin, the restaurant didn't have a knife sharp enough to cut the steaks. We went over Donner Pass and re-lived the story of the Donner Party's cannibalism and even experienced snow on the mountain peaks. We dropped into the Sacramento Valley where my aunt lived. My uncle had died a couple of years before when we were in Europe. He woke up one morning got ready for work, got dressed and went to his office where he had a massive heart attack and died. We had not been home for several years.

After a couple of days we drove to San Francisco to visit my grandparents. If I remember correctly I had to spend a couple of days with my aunt and uncle in Walnut Creek California and then back to my grandparents. During that period of time the folks went to Pacific Grove to look for housing. We bought a house in Pacific Grove California and moved in.

Dad went to Viet Nam and came home when he could He also took our 1955 Chevy with him to drive until the end of his assignment, and sell on the local market when he got transferred back to the states. The car was distinctive; it was a two tone, painted coral (pink) on the bottom and gun metal gray on the top. Our replacement car was a brand new 1958 yellow Chevy which turned out to be the world's biggest lemon. It's a good thing that it was yellow. I'm not kidding when I say that the day we picked up the car we went for a fifteen mile ride in it and the fuel pump went out. It spent more time behind a tow truck than on its own power.

I was sixteen, in High School and trying to get along in a civilian environment. The civilian culture was completely foreign to me, and I didn't like it. Mom was the person who suffered the most. She had to do all of the work in running a house and be a single parent. Her health suffered and something had to be done to protect her. I don't know who contacted dad but it was explained how serious her condition was. At this point she had lived as a single parent for a substantial period of her married life, seven out of the nineteen years she and dad were married. It was decided hot zone or not, mom would move to Saigon, I would go over there for at least the summer, and then if necessary come back to Pacific Grove to finish high school and live with my paternal grandmother, who had moved to Pacific Grove. I should point out that I never did get along with her.

After all the necessary arrangements were made we were going to Viet Nam. Mom had accepted the necessity of flying there since Viet Nam was 10,000 miles away. Mom didn't have any experience with flying and was nervous. The trip took about five days from San Francisco to Saigon on Pan American's Clipper Service with stops in Hawaii, Wake Island, Manila and then on to Saigon. The plane was the Pan American Stratocruiser, the Boeing 377, nicknamed the guppy. The lower deck was fitted out as a lounge with the seats on the upper level. It was a very comfortable airplane, made even so much more with the travelling businessmen drinking free booze in the lounge and never sleeping, which left more room for us on the upper level. The food was excellent and seemed to be prepared right on the plane. Those were the days when Pan Am not only operated the airline but owned the food service vendors and prepared the food; and owned the hotels used for layovers. You could get an excellent Filet Mignon and baked potato served very hot; and of course beaucoup Champaign. The stewardess would bring the magnum bottles through the passenger compartment every few minutes. The passenger seats were large and comfortable about the size of first class seats today. There was plenty of legroom to stretch out and some of the planes had sleeping berths. The only thing on the negative side of the equation is that there was vibration throughout the plane because of the four propeller engines. You did get used to the vibration.

Its 1958 and I'm seventeen and mom is watching me like a hawk to make sure that I don't find my way to the lounge. I do get champagne from the stewardess on a regular basis.

THE CAMP FOLLOWER

We take off from San Francisco at midnight bound for Hawaii, landing in Honolulu at about eight in the morning. We have a couple of hours before our next flight takes off so I get a haircut before dad sees my hair. My hair has always been a bone of contention with him because it was thick and curly, so I usually ended up with a flattop cut by an army barber. I used to envy those people who could actually comb their hair and make it look good. I think it took about four minutes to get my hair cut by the army barber, so it was a treat for me to get a haircut that took fifteen or twenty minutes.

Our next stop is Wake Island. It's nothing but a flat sandbox. All I wanted to do was stretch my legs, so I started walking around the island. All there seems to be is the runway and a pseudo terminal. While I was walking I couldn't help but think how the war got here. It's flat, little vegetation and more importantly no place to hide.

From Wake we flew to Manila. Pan Am checked all of the passengers into its layover hotel so that we could have some privacy, take a shower, lay on a real bed, etc. Pan Am took care of its passengers to the point where they were spoiled from the attention. With today's airline service I won't get on a plane unless it's an emergency. Believe me, there was no comparison with the cattle cars of today.

We arrive at Tan Son Nhut Airport in Saigon, the plane stopping on the tarmac. When the airline crew opens the door to disembark the passengers you can feel a stream of hot air coming from the door. By the time I got to the plane's door it was like walking into a hot oven. I immediately start perspiring before I reach the bottom of the steps. I want to get back on the plane and go somewhere else. Just like most airports the area adjacent to the airport is pretty desolate. Dad picks us up in the '55 Chevy. We get in the car and take off for the house dad had gotten for us. The parts of Saigon we drive through are really not too impressive, kind of bare. Not at all like the nickname the city has; "The Paris of the Orient". You can tell that the natives are living in an economy that is not middle class. Our house is a typical French Colonial three story concrete house. It has a courtyard and four bungalows at the back of the house for the servants. It's pretty easy to tell that the French have been living rather well just like they have done in any of the other countries they have colonized with no regard for human rights. The first floor of the house is the family area with the family room, kitchen, pantries, etc. The second floor is the formal common area, living room and formal dining room. The bedrooms are on the third floor. The first floor and the master bedroom are air conditioned. My bedroom is not air conditioned, but I'm only there for the summer anyway. Besides the monsoon is approaching and the rain will drive some of the heat away. My bed has a mosquito net over it, I'm sure that will come in handy. Glass windows are not used so there are metal jealousies. The walls and ceiling are full of Geckos running around and I am told that they are my friends because they eat mosquitoes.

The next thing is dad's briefing to me. He tells me that he is on the Viet Cong's death list and I will probably be included as a way to get to him. I should be extra careful if I am wandering around the city.

There were preventive measures to be taken with regard to health. First thing in the morning we were expected to take

THE CAMP FOLLOWER

a salt pill that was fairly large, and a quinine pill to prevent malaria. Of course the more important was the quinine since malaria scared the shit out of me.

He also gives me a short course in Vietnamese law which specifies that if someone breaks into your house, you have the right to fight him with the same weapon that he is using. So if he has a stick the only thing you can use is a stick, etc, etc. Also the car will have a driver; no Drivers License will be given to mom or me.

Kim was the driver that was hired; he seemed to come out of nowhere, don't know if he had any defensive driving training. He sure liked our 1955 Chevy because of its power and proved it on a couple of occasions when I was riding with him. Since Kim was in the Vietnamese army in the 1954 war and his proficiency at driving is more than just competent, I'm guessing that he does have defensive driving experience.

The folks got the word out that we were looking for a couple to cook and act as housekeeper. We did get a couple, he was an excellent chef and she was a very good housekeeper. Mom didn't complain about her and mom was quite fussy about the housekeeping.

There was another Kim; he had been dad's houseboy for the past year. He was helpful, friendly and a real asset to the family since he acted as the family interpreter. Everything pointed to us having a spy among us, but we thought it was the cook. After the whole family got back to the states we heard that Kim was accused of being a Viet Cong spy. Talk about Clue, where's Colonel Mustard! I certainly hope that nothing happened to Kim; he did help me a lot and even saved the sight in my right eye.

That finished the staffing of the house. I was introduced to some of the American teenagers in Saigon. The guys always went to the Club Sportief in the morning at about ten o'clock. The club was the country club in Saigon and had a large swimming pool. This is where the French plantation managers new trophy wives and mistresses would hang out. It seems that these women didn't like plantation life. They all wore white cotton bikinis and exactly at eleven would jump into the pool. They would spend a couple of minutes in the pool splashing around and then they would all get out. This, for all intents and purposes, made their swimming suits transparent. I often thought they were doing that for our benefit or spite; can you imagine what effect that had on us seventeen year old healthy males?

The cook had become established at the local markets and got to know the kitchen and what he could do in it. He fixed his first lunch. We were all blown away when he served a platter of crayfish the size of small lobsters. I don't know if they were named crayfish or langoustines. All I know is that with drawn butter they were delicious; and given the fact that there was a platter of fresh native fruit on the table, lunch was complete.

We went to tour and countryside and the Saigon River. Dad borrowed a speedboat for the river and one of the things that I noticed is that there were a number of eighteen foot fiberglass boat hulls on the banks. There were no outboard engines to be seen. I asked dad what the boat hulls were doing there and he said that the French used them for landing craft. To my mind

Mom driving Converted French Landing Craft

these were the worst landing craft you could imagine. They had sharp bows and at best one or two people could get off the boat at once. Closer inspection of the hulls revealed that they were made by the Wizard Boat Company of Los Angeles. I guess that if you're going to support somebody like the French, you might as well give them something that can be re-cycled.

Dad was able to get one of he hulls, got an outboard engine and sent the hull over to the boat builder at the Club Nautique. The boat builder installed good seats, installed a mahogany deck, dashboard, steering, controls and painted it and made it look like a handsome run-a-bout. It was moored at the Club Nautique and now we had our own boat, although we used it infrequently while I was there.

We drove up Highway One which was a two lane paved highway with forests on either side. I'm in Eden; there are Peacocks on the side of the road. Highway One has so many mourning doves on it sunning themselves you couldn't count them. That with the snakes, all sizes of cats, deer and all the other exotic animals made this the closest thing to the biblical description of what I imagined to be the Garden of Eden. In the North they even had wild elephants; there was more life there than I could imagine. I imagine that was due to the counties religious tradition in the countryside. In excess of eighty percent of the people were Buddhist. The religious minority lived in Saigon. President Diem was Catholic and supported the church to excess.

Kim, the driver, wants me to go with him for a ride. I'm sure that I'm the excuse, but OK we go out. We are going through the better residential sections of Saigon; there is very

THE CAMP FOLLOWER

little automobile or pedestrian traffic. Kim is driving very fast and won't slow down. When dad gets home that night, he starts giving me hell for driving that fast in Saigon. I didn't lay it off on Kim because I really liked him so I took the anger, besides that I was used to it after all those years. Then dad starts describing our route. I could see someone noticing that pink and gray bomb tearing through the city streets, but knowing our route is a different animal altogether. We were being followed! At this point my imagination kicks in, who would want to follow us? I start visualizing the procession. First of course that two tone Chevy, no one knew who was in the car; followed by a Viet Cong operative riding a moped, next we come to the CIA operative probably driving a Citroen-2CV; followed; in turn by a Vietnamese secret police operative driving a Citroen DS and finally a French intelligence operative driving a petticab and pedaling like hell. The Vietnamese secret police didn't trust the CIA. That's as good as any comedy movie from the sixties.

The next foray into what I think was the intelligence community was my date with the Quartermaster's daughter. There was a rumor that the Quartermaster was actually the officer in charge of CIA's covert operations. The thing in the back of my mind was that we were all living off the local economy and the commissary was small. I didn't understand why we needed a senior Quartermaster? Anyway his daughter was very attractive and had a good personality. We went to the movies. I wasn't allowed to have Kim, the driver, and the car so we took a Citroen-2CV taxicab. The-2CV is about the size of the Morris Minor we had in Europe so it was easy to get close, if you know what I mean. On the way home we are necking like crazy and having a good time when she says

"Mom is going to the commissary in the morning, so why don't you come over about 10". Being seventeen and stupid I didn't get her address and even though I saw their house, I was too busy necking to remember how to get there the next morning. So the next morning I get a cab and we start looking for a house with no address or directions. I'm yelling to the cab driver "Go down this street" and "Try that one over there". You have to remember that I'm speaking in pigeon French and the cab driver is getting confused. If that girl is reading this, I apologize. Then I start thinking that if her father was a spook, was she a spook too?

    I had always fantasized about big game hunting and read all of the outdoor magazines. I could imagine myself standing up to an elephant or lion and coming back victorious, so I wanted to go tiger hunting. Viet Nam was a favorite of Hemingway's and in my book he was one of the greatest big game hunters in the world. We stayed at the rubber plantation houses, which were no castles and hunt at night. Hunting for big cats was kind of interesting if not totally terrorizing. You needed a jeep with at least three men. The backstop had a 30-06 rifle and stayed in the jeep. Then there was the driver, our Kim was the driver naturally, and the hunters. The hunters had modified twelve gauge shotguns loaded with double naught buckshot. You started on the hunt between midnight and one o'clock in the morning by cruising the roads in the area you were hunting. The cats would not be on the roads but in the brush and fields adjacent to the roads. You can smell the cat's markings from long distances and that smell is just like jumping into a bottle of cat urine. In the jeep you have a very high power searchlight and each of the hunters has a miner's lamp on his forehead. After you smell the cat's marking you start searching with the high power searchlight. When you catch the animal's eyes in the searchlight, it mesmerizes them. The hunter, one only, gets out of the jeep with his shotgun and starts walking toward the eyes. When the hunter gets closer than forty yards of the cat he turns on his headlamp and signals the jeep to turn off the searchlight. After the jeep searchlight goes off the hunter attracts the attention of the cat with his headlamp. When he gets the cat's attention he continues walking toward the animal until he feels comfortable enough to complete the kill. He then fires and hopefully kills the animal. If he doesn't he still has three more shells and chances to kill the animal or run like hell. I shot a panther like that and I can tell you I have never been so frightened in my life. The cat was mortally wounded but not dead. I had completed my third manhood test. Nobody can say I'm not a man. I remember going back to the jeep, backing up part of the way and turning around when I tripped over something. I wished I could fly. Those one hundred yards were the longest walk of my life.

The strange thing about our hunting trips is shortly after we decide where to go on the trip; the Viet Cong move into the area and bivouac at the plantation showing a presence. I don't know of any violence during this period to either the natives working on the plantations or to the plantation management, I don't think there was any. We usually arrive late Friday afternoon and the Viet Cong will have moved out of the area in the morning of that day. That's what gave us the clue that someone in our house was broadcasting our travel plans.

Someone gives dad a Mynah Bird. The bird is one hateful creature sitting there and spiting at anyone who passes by. The bird never did learn to talk, at least not while I was there.

Mynah Birds eat hot peppers. In fact the hotter the pepper the better they like it. There was a little green pepper that was so hot that it would burn your skin to the point of blistering. I was walking beside the bird's cage when it spit pepper juice into my right eye. In a microsecond it started burning my eye. The pain was unbearable and I couldn't get the juice out of my eye. Kim, the houseboy, saw the pain I was in and quickly came to my aid. He directed me to the bathroom and told me to take off my left shoe. I argued that it was my right eye, not my left foot. He finally convinced me to take off my left shoe and sock. He then had me put my left foot in the lavatory basin; he turned the cold water on and started massaging my big left toe with the water. To my amazement in a couple of minutes I was no longer in pain nor could I feel any affects of the pepper juice. I guess that proves that ancient medicines are real and we in the occidental world can learn immense information about ourselves and the treatments of our ailments.

I asked dad if we could go up to the Vietnamese highlands so I can meet some Montagnard tribesmen that he knows. The Montagnards are said to be the original indigenous people of Viet Nam. The Chinese invaded and took over the country becoming the dominant people. The Montagnards live a traditional lifestyle, living in the jungle usually next to a river. The village is centered on a family unit. They are excellent hunters and trackers, during the Vietnamese war the US Special Forces used them a great deal for fighting the Viet Cong and North Vietnamese Army. This particular village is next to a small rubber plantation and had a Catholic missionary in the area. The plantation people and the missionary entertained us throughout the morning. There is a rushing river between the plantation house and the village. When I say rushing I really

Montagnard Chief

mean it, this river looks like a rapid. We have been invited to the village and some of the young villagers have paddled their dugout canoes over to the plantation side of the river to give us a ride back to their side of the river. Yep, I said dugout canoes. I didn't see the canoes approaching the shore, but that's understandable. They started from the other side about a quarter mile upstream. I'm looking at the river, the current, the villagers who don't look that strong and the dugout canoes. The only saving thought that I had is when I drown today it will be all dads' fault and mom will never forgive him. We walk up river about a quarter of a mile, get into the canoes while the tribesmen push us off from the bank; and I smile because I have been through the manhood thing already and I didn't want anyone to know I was scared shitless.

The village is a concentration of bamboo huts, some for people and some for livestock. The huts are raised off the ground for protection against wild things like snakes. It looks like most of the livestock are chickens. The village people are trading with the plantation people and the missionary but I don't know what goods they are trading. The Montagnards believe in plural marriages so the headman is usually the father or grandfather of most of the people in the village. By this time I have a new camera, a twin lens Yashica. I'm having the time of my life taking pictures of the village and soaking up this culture. Sometime in the past we all lived like this and it's interesting to see people living like this out of choice in a modern society. We drive back to Saigon with the feeling that the summer was almost over.

My folks had discussed it and I was going back to Pacific Grove. I could get into too much trouble in Saigon and I would

Montagnard Village

have to take correspondence courses from UC Berkeley to finish high school.

One of the places that I really wanted to see was Angkor Wat. From everything I've seen in the pictures it is better than any Greek or Roman antiquity. It's all there, nothing like the Roman Coliseum where people have been stealing it for decades. We never did get the opportunity to go and I guess that Cambodia was even more dangerous than Viet Nam.

For the rest of my time in Saigon I am running around with the surviving seventeen year olds. We are drinking Mum's Champaign at US $3.50 a bottle, smoking Filipino cigars and playing Poker. Might as well go home, I'm getting bored. One of the guys was kicked out of the country, multiple cases of syphilis. He swore he didn't have sex while he was there; obviously he had more fun than I did. There is one more place I should mention, it was on the main drag in Saigon and it made the best cheeseburgers you could imagine. It also made delicious milkshakes. Now, I don't know what kind of meat I was eating or if the milk was pasteurized but it was sure good. The owner had spent a few years in New York City; and finally returned to Viet Nam.

Another diversion for our little group was to go to the movies in the basement of the British Embassy. That was kind of interesting since it seems to me that the only movies we saw were British wartime movies and the British always won. If there were any allies, they weren't very evident. The thing I had to get used to was at the end of the movie a special segment was added at which time you were expected to stand almost at attention while the picture projected on the screen was

THE CAMP FOLLOWER

Queen Elizabeth, the British flag and the audio playing "God save the Queen". That took a little getting used to, being a good American.

Its time to go home, so dad arranged my flight. Since he knows that this is a lifetime opportunity for me, he sets my itinerary to maximize the experience. I will be flying from Saigon to Bangkok, to Manila, to Tokyo, to Hong Kong; and then start the trip back to the states. That includes Hong Kong to Manila, to Wake Island, to Honolulu and then on to San Francisco.

My parents didn't know it but they were about to make the worst decision of their lives. I am travelling alone to all these exotic places with money in my pocket. I'm even worried that I won't show up in San Francisco anytime soon. I have two minds about leaving Viet Nam, I love it here. I guess I've got to go, the decision has been made and I don't have too much to say about it.

We all go out to Tan Son Nhut on the day of the flight. Mom is crying as we approach the plane and dad is looking stoic. As we get near the plane dad tells me to say a final goodbye to mom and then come back to him. Mom is crying so hard that I want to cry too, but I don't! When I get back to dad, he gives me a wad of cash which is equal to several hundred dollars, close to a thousand. Of course I need to be lectured not to squander the money and to keep it safe. His other instructions were to have some nice clothes made in Hong Kong, but not to buy anything frivolous like a tux. He also told me that I had a five day layover in Hong Kong and a three day layover in Hawaii. The person I was supposed to stay with in Hong Kong was Willie Wong and I was to stay at the Bachelors Officers Quarters at Fort Derussy in Hawaii. He suggested that it didn't matter how long this trip took me as long as I got back in time for the first day of school; and I was to notify the aunt who was supposed to pick me up at the airport when I arrived. I was to call her from Hawaii to give her time to arrange her trip to the airport. She lived in Walnut Creek which is about forty miles from San Francisco.

Off I go to Bangkok. We arrive; I check into a hotel and go out sightseeing in the city. I want to leave the next day so I change my reservations. I really don't have the time to spend more time here, besides the city doesn't look that interesting to me. I wander into an antique shop and look at a hand carved ivory chess set that's supposed to be at least a hundred years old. Now that I'm responsible for myself, even though the set was very attractive, good sense prevailed and I figured that the set was made yesterday from plastic. In retrospect the set was probably ivory and probably two hundred years old. That's just my luck. I went back to the hotel and looked in the shops in the lobby area. There was an American guy following me around the lobby. I couldn't shake him so I went into the men's room. He followed me and when I was standing at the urinal he reached inside my pants. Didn't take me long to react. When I left the men's room, he was still on the floor. I decided my hotel room was as good as any place to stay until dinner time.

The next morning I went back to the airport. I decided to get my grandparents something more than a trinket, so I went to the duty free liquor store and bought six bottles of Bushmills Irish Whiskey. I was told the familiar story "the bottles will be on the plane" which was OK by me.

THE CAMP FOLLOWER

I fly to Manila where I buy a couple of boxes of Philippine cigars for my grandfather. Not much to do there so I decide to catch the next flight to Tokyo.

The flight is uneventful, although there are two young American women on the flight who seem to be interested in me. We arrive in Tokyo and go to the customs area. The customs officer tells me that I can't take the Whiskey into the country, even with my Special Passport, without paying a very heavy duty. He didn't recommend that; I asked him what my options were trying to be as sophisticated as possible. He finally admits that the booze could go into storage until I leave the country for a nominal rental fee. He sure wanted that booze, I gave him the flight number I would be leaving the country on and paid the rent and got a signed receipt. I could pick up the booze at the gate before boarding the plane. I boarded the shuttle bus. The driver asks which hotel I want to go to and I mistakenly tell him the wrong hotel. The two girls said they wanted to go to the same hotel. By that time I had realized my mistake and corrected it. The girls didn't hear me correct myself, so goodbye girls. One of the things I really wanted to try while in Tokyo was the Kobe beef. I settled in the hotel, changed my clothes and then went to get my steak. I got a cab, told the driver that I wanted to go to a restaurant that served Kobe beef and off we go. We end up on a side street with the driver trying to convince me that the restaurant we had stopped at served my beef. Now I don't know whether his definition of steak was different than mine or he was getting a commission from the bar owner, but I ended up in a bar and whorehouse. The girls are awfully nice so I had a couple of beers. Never did get my steak. Off I go to Hong Kong.

Hong Kong in the 1950's before the Viet Nam war was an amazing place. I arrive at about two in the afternoon, get a cab and go over to Willie's apartment. I am met at Willie's front door by his housekeeper who doesn't speak any English. Willie must have worked the late shift the night before because he is not up yet. Willie works for Cathay Airlines. It's obvious that he doesn't know anything about my arrival but he takes that in stride and invites me in. We talked for a while, he showed me a bedroom I could use and we started planning my stay. It turned out to be a most interesting stay I could imagine. Willie's father was one of the most prominent businessmen in Saigon and had regular dealings with my father. So what I could imagine is that if we did anything exotic Willie would mention it to his father who would in turn mention it to my father who would accuse me of squandering the money; and of course, the inverse would be true on Willies part with the exception of squandering the money. Fathers are not "on a need to know" basis. Anyway Willie takes me to a Dim Sum restaurant for a late lunch and then on to his favorite tailor for me to pick out some clothes and have measurements taken.

The rules for my stay are simple. We breakfast at approximately three in the afternoon go out for dinner at about ten, hang out watching shows in the clubs until closing at midnight and then on to the after hours clubs. The after hours clubs close down in the morning. We should arrive home at about three in the morning. Between breakfast and dinner we will see the sights of Hong Kong. There are some exceptions to the rule and those include my fittings at the tailor, any road trips like to the peninsula and haircuts. Included with the haircuts are manicures.

THE CAMP FOLLOWER

Willie had been invited to the eighth birthday of a distant relative. I guess he asked if he could bring me along. I politely tried to back out. Willie tells me that he has already accepted in my name and not to go would be an insult. OK we go to the dinner; as a matter of fact I'm looking forward to it. Willie tells me that not to insult the old lady we have to stay for a certain number of courses. I can't remember if it was six or sixteen. I remember sixteen but that might be the result of a senior moment. Her family was celebrating her eightieth birthday and thus the banquet. We ate at one long table in the Asian tradition. The food started coming with my favorite Sharks fin soup first. I can't remember how many courses I ate but I do remember that Willie had to drag me out of there. Every course was better than the previous. Let's just say that I exceeded the minimum number of courses by a bunch.

I'm seeing Hong Kong unlike any tourist sees it, and my guide is willing and able to show it to me. We take sampans to floating restaurants in the bay. We go to the Tigarbaum Gardens which is interesting and has the best view of Hong Kong and the peninsula on the island. The Tigarbaum Gardens are a series of sculptures adjacent to a path on the top of a mountain. The figures in the sculpture are of jungle animals in three dimensions on the side of the wall.

Willie and Hong Kong made the trip worth it and will be one of the most valuable memories in my lifetime and never forgotten. I pick up my clothes, buy a nice leather suitcase to put them in and get ready to leave. By the way, the clothes included a tux. Off I go to Wake Island and then on to Honolulu.

I arrive in Honolulu; check in to the Fort Derussy Bachelor Officers Quarters which costs me one dollar a night. I am exhausted, tired of airplanes and just want to go home. You can't believe how much attention a seventeen year old got travelling around the Orient by himself in the fifties. I call my aunt and tell her my estimated time of arrival in San Francisco. I was supposed to meet some friends from Saigon and go to the movies that night. I took a walk on the beach and couldn't help noticing how much better the beach was in the Derussy base than the beach at the Reef Hotel next door. I took a nap and when I woke up I didn't know what day it was. I did make it to the movies. Next day I boarded the flight to San Francisco. I knew that this leg of the trip would probably be my last foreign adventure in my lifetime. The belief that this would be my last foreign trip turned out not to be the case because my career took me to many foreign places.

GOING HOME

We arrived in San Francisco at about two in the afternoon. It seemed like it had been a lifetime since I had been in San Francisco and I had completely changed. I didn't even recognize my grandparents for a couple of seconds. Finally recognizing all of the family that had come to pick me up, I got with the program and hugged everyone. The group was comprised of my grandparents and my aunt and uncle. After all the hellos were said my uncle looked me straight in the eye and said "Have I got a surprise for you", of course I responded what? He again looked me straight in the eye and responded "We're going down to Chinatown for a good Chinese dinner". Well gee, I am looking forward to Chinese food and off we went. After dinner I was given the option of staying at my grandparents or going to my aunt and uncle's house. I choose my grandparents since I still had that suitcase full of Irish whiskey and cigars. My aunt and uncle left finally and I proceeded to deliver my goods. My grandfather was very appreciative of the gifts; my grandmother looked at the Irish whiskey and all she said was "We won't drink that shit". My grandfather tried to calm her down and explain to me why the outcry. It turns out that Bushmills is distilled in Northern Ireland. If you are going to drink Irish it has to be Jameson's, at least in their house. They immigrated to the US before Southern Ireland was given its independence from England and she still held a grudge against the English and the Protestant Northern Irish. I think that she wanted to start her own war of re-unification; it was a topic of conversation for those Irish immigrants in San Francisco who came over at the turn of the century. I'm probably related to most of them.

After dad retired from the army, the government of Viet Nam offered him a job being a liaison between Viet Nam and the United States. He thought about it for a while but the FBI warned him against it. It almost sounds like the FBI knew that there was a major conflict in the making.

AT HOME

I spent a couple of days with my grandparents, and of course, my aunt and uncle insisted that I visit with them for a couple of days. The school year was about to start and I still had to get down to Pacific Grove and see if I could reach an agreement with my paternal grandmother on the rules of her house. I was sure that she wanted to control me while I was staying there, and that was unacceptable. So I jumped on a Greyhound bus for the ride down to Pacific Grove. I would have preferred to take the train the "Del Monte Special" which was an old line train from San Francisco to Pacific Grove where it deadheaded for the night. It was a fun train, a commuter train from San Francisco to San Jose and then it became an express, which went too slow to be an express. Anyway I would have had to travel to San Francisco to get the train, so I decided to take the bus.

After arriving in Pacific Grove I took a cab over to my Grandmother's house since it was a mile or so and I still had a bunch of suitcases. In a letter a little more than a week later my mother expressed the concern that it seemed to my grandmother that it was extravagant for me to have taken a cab. That also gave me a good indication what I was up against. I would keep my own counsel and start planning my escape.

This went on for a couple of months and I hated everything about living there from the TV programs she watched to her dogs, and I gave her one of the dogs. Both dogs had come from our family. She ruined them. They were never housebroken! The puppy I gave her had a great personality which was lost and gone forever.

Pacific Grove was a town where the taxis ran booze into the town, because by ordinance, it was dry. The way it worked was that you would call the cab company and give them your booze order. The cab would then go to the liquor store and buy the liquor for you, take it to your destination, and you would pay for the booze and the cab ride. The reason the town was dry was because it started out as a religious camp and the town fathers considered booze the devils tool. I wonder what the town fathers would have thought seeing all of those cabs running up and down the streets in the middle of the night. The town fathers missed the boat; they made selling liquor against the law but didn't enact a law prohibiting drinking the stuff. Sounds like the Midwest.

One of the guys in my class in high school had an extra bed in his bedroom so I decided to see if we were compatible enough to live together and if his mother would like some extra cash. I talked to my mother about it by phone and she was agreeable. There was no love lost between my mother and grandmother. This guy and I had hung out together since we had moved to Pacific Grove. The deal was set, I moved into their house. I think that made my grandmother supremely happy and was the worst decision that could be made for my future. Now I had minimal to no adult supervision and was going wild. I can't describe the ways I screwed up but it doesn't leave much to the imagination.

THE CAMP FOLLOWER

Once I remember that my roommate decided to have a party. His grandmother was going out of town for a few days and we would use her house, without her permission. All of the party supplies were acquired and the party started. I think that it was the next door neighbor who saw all the cars on the street and the noise and lights coming from the house, and knowing that the house was supposed to be empty, called the police. The police showed up and busted us for breaking in and of course having alcohol on the premises. The police told the girls that showed up to the party to go home, which left us guys to face the music. Off we went to the police station where the desk sergeant told us that he would notify our parents so they can come and pick us up. One by one we were to stand up and answer the sergeant's questions. It was finally my turn and I got up, the sergeant asked me for my parent's phone number. Its decision time for me, I have to try a lengthy explanation or just give him the phone number in Saigon. I decide on the Saigon number. He responds that is not a valid number and I explain that it is in Saigon. He wants to know where Saigon is and I tell him it is in Viet Nam. He wants to know where Viet Nam is and I point to the west and say ten thousand miles that way; and dad was a Colonel in the army. The poor guy was so frustrated he decided to let us go, he knew that I am being truthful since the rest of my group agreed with everything I said. He told us to walk home, do not get into our cars, and pick up the cars tomorrow. The sergeant didn't want us to drink and drive, but we hadn't had anything to drink. We went back to the cars and drove home.

My parents are coming home and I can't wait to see them even though I'm sure that there will be a time in purgatory, if not hell. Dad is retiring and decided to go into Real Estate.

That seemed to be the natural thing to do considering all of the military bases on the Monterey Peninsula. Since he was going to be a retired Colonel, his rank gave him a leg up. All he had to do was study for the Real Estate Salesmans Test and find and get hired by a friendly broker. It wasn't much of a problem to find a friendly broker. While I was waiting for the folks to come home I heard about Kalisa's Restaurant on Cannery Row.

I met Kalisa shortly after she opened her restaurant on Cannery Row, in what I remember as 1959. I became interested in her restaurant when I heard that she didn't pursue a carding policy for wine and beer. It was my kind of place since I was only eighteen. The people who were the most likely to become good customers were soldiers from the Army Language School, the artsy crowd from Monterey, including well-known painters and photographers, folk singers, jazz musicians, people like me who were looking for an environment where they could feel comfortable, the occasional solder from Fort Ord on a pass, and one wine-maker who worked in the Salinas Valley for a well-known winery The soldiers were very important to us male teenagers; they could buy liquor from the liquor stores without much trouble. The closest liquor store was about two blocks away. We bartered on the basis that they would buy the beer, we would pay the soldiers for it, and when they were ready we would drive them back to the Army Language School or Fort Ord, which in the case of Fort Ord would save them about an hour with the connecting buses. Most of the time we let the solders out at the front gate and they could make their way back to their barracks. We always had a designated driver for this task. We were a pretty conservative lot.

That was before Cannery Row had become commercialized. The street was still processing fish occasionally, so it still stank

THE CAMP FOLLOWER

at times, and the Steinbeck bums were still living in the boiler plate. Doc's lab had become an exclusive men's club. I don't know what changes had been made to the inside primarily because my only description of the lab was Steinbeck's. I had never been inside the building. The outside of the building was naturally weathered to match the rest of the street with no effort by the members to improve the building's appearance

Dad had a boat made in Hong Kong on the folk's way back to the U.S. It was a mahogany constructed clinker hull of eighteen feet. It was a beautiful riding hull, but we still got into more trouble than you can imagine. Let's just say that the Coast Guard got tired of giving us tickets and just let us off with warnings.

Dad would study for his real estate test on the boat while he was fishing. So he would go out into the bay, do a little bottom fishing and study. It was working out well for him since he could study undisturbed and catch some good cod and other bottom fish. At that time the bay was good fishing. You could catch twenty or thirty pounds of fish in no time. You would take your catch to Fisherman's Warf to have them filleted. That cost approximately two or three cents a pound. During Salmon season you would see a couple of hundred boats on the bay, and most limiting out on Salmon. Storm warning flags didn't mean too much to us.

We took a fishing trip where you couldn't see the land except briefly at the top of the trough; all you could see for any period of time was the bottom of the trough and the overcast sky. I think that the ground swells were about fifteen feet. The bow of the boat would submerge into the bottom of the swell almost up to the windshield and then pop up.

That was the second time dad wanted adult advice from me on what to do; the first time had been about the transfer to the Air Force. I didn't know what to do. I was standing at the windshield hanging on to the foredeck. Neither of us could sit down because we would have been thrown out. The conditions were brutal and I seriously doubted if we could turn the boat a hundred and eighty degrees and then head for home. Now you've got to understand that if we both drowned on this trip, I couldn't blame it on dad like in the Vietnamese Highlands. So my suggestion was to head to the top of the trough and when we almost to the top turn this sucker around really hard with our life vests on, just in case we brought them. We got home safely and hoisted the boat into the warehouse, then went home. Neither of us spoke of that experience again except to say that it was really rough out there.

We got tired of the sharks stealing our stringers of fish while we were bottom fishing. By that time I had an over and under rifle shotgun combination. Of course the rifle was a twenty two and the shotgun was a four ten gauge. Somebody told dad how to attract a shark. So we fixed up a bait to be towed it from the back of the boat. We finally see a dorsal fin off in the distance. It didn't take long for the shark to close on the bait. The bait was about fifty feet from the stern. I was pulling the bait closer to the boat and dad was hunched at the transom with the gun. When the shark got to the transom, it lifted its head over the transom, dad got up and shot him between the eyes with a shotgun shell and then followed it with the bullet. The shark started making backward spirals into the deep. When we got back to the dock and were telling our story to the local fishermen, their only comment was that it was a good thing that we didn't piss off the shark.

THE CAMP FOLLOWER

There were a few commercial improvements made to the Cannery Row neighborhood. One of the canneries had been converted to a storage building specializing in boat storage. It was kind of interesting since the floor level on the storage area was about thirty feet from the water. So what you had to do to access the water was to lower and raise your boat with the crane that had been used for unloading sardines from the fishing boats. That warehouse was where our boat was housed.

Kalisa's building had been the "Bear Flag Inn" during Steinbeck's Cannery Row days. Steinbeck made the building famous or infamous since he described it as the whorehouse on the street. The building had deteriorated by the late fifties but it was still a beautiful place as far as I was concerned. There was a restaurant next door that had named itself the Bear Flag Inn to take advantage of the Steinbeck connection, but I don't think it was ever very popular. Kalisa's building was the real thing, you could tell since it still had the outbuilding in the rear of the property. The outbuilding consisted of bedrooms numbered one through six which were definitely designed to short term use. Each room had a bed, lavatory, and a nightstand. There was one bathroom for the building.

Kalisa arranged the main building with a bar on the first floor, kitchen and dining room on the second floor; with a private room at the back of that floor. This was simply the first iteration of many, and I was involved in a lot of them.

There were three places I would hang out. The first was Kalisa's for obvious reasons. The second was a European style sandwich restaurant in Monterey called Sancho Panza's where you could get an excellent sandwich with a frappuccino for lunch. The third place was a coffee house across from Lovers Point in Pacific Grove during the Jack Kerouac period. This was for early evenings since most of the people that went there were truly beatniks and their weird poetry got boring pretty easily.

Kalisa's was a family affair. Her father who carried himself like a 19th century aristocrat, greeted the customers at the front door and was the mater'd. We would all stand around when the place was quiet trying to figure out if her father was a Russian or a German officer during the war. Her mother was the cook. The fare was European, but not tourist European; and it definitely had a unique taste. Kalisa would be marketing to almost everyone that came into the restaurant. After the dinner hour the bar became filled with either folk singing or jazz. There was real art hanging on the walls on loan from the artists who were the regulars. They could sell their art in the restaurant if someone was interested in buying it. I bought a really nice figure study from the photographer for about twenty dollars.

The greatest improvement to the street at that time was the best restaurant on the Monterey Peninsula. The name of the restaurant was Neal Devon's. As I recall the restaurants access to the street was a weathered wooden door going from the grungy Cannery Row street scene to an elegant bar and restaurant with a small main dining room overlooking the bay and the wait staff in tuxedoes or black skirts and white blouses. The waiters and waitresses had a work load of two tables apiece. The service was exceptional and the wait staff didn't have to worry about under tipping. The place was always packed with customers. I did realize and appreciated the fact that I had been given the opportunity to taste both sides of life on Cannery Row, and enjoyed both of them.

The developers were about to commercialize the street. The safest thing to do was to build something that would have appeal to the locals. That became the Steinbeck Plaza on the seaward side of the street. It consisted of a movie theatre aptly named The Steinbeck and store fronts from the theatre back to the street. They even put a metal sculpture in this plaza, can't remember if it was Steinbeck or not. The next thing was a restaurant across from the movie theater was called the Outrigger. The Outrigger was a tourist trap, plain and simple. You could buy Cannery Row souvenirs at the entrance to the building. That opened the floodgates. At the end of the street was a theatre, or something like a theatre, that blasted out "In a godda da vita" continuously from their front door to Kalisa's across the street. I paid to see the performance once and was surprised when I got inside and saw an empty stage with the song playing a little louder. If I concentrate I can still hear it in my mind. I should have stayed outside and listened from there for free. Then the warehouse half a block away and up one street was converted into a spaghetti factory, and on and on it went.

The City finally got involved and turned the empty lots with the boilerplates into parking lots with parking meters. That displaced the bums. The whole thing had become Disneyland on Monterey Bay. Finally hotels were built where fisherman's houses had stood. It had become the place for merchants to relieve the tourists of their money. Before that happened there were some very good times had by us, the denizens of the street. Steinbeck was right in his approach to humanity. The people he wrote about were the people we wanted to be. We had fun.

Before the explosion of commercialization of the street I was heavily involved in Kalisa's. Kalisa never got along with the City fathers. They made her tear down the backhouse because they considered it old and unsightly, with no consideration to its historical value. You couldn't see it from the street, or the adjacent street. They inspected her building without notice and found that the building foundations needed reinforcement. I remember that her dad was jacking up the building so he could strengthen the foundation. He was about seventy then, and for the most part refused any help from us. In the end Kalisa's nemeses on the City Council died before Kalisa, so I guess she won.

Now you have to realize that Kalisa was never commercially successful in her fifty odd years in business in Monterey, but she added humanity to the community. Everyone in Monterey knew of her. Her dress was always a muumuu. I think that her style of dressing was that she needed a maternity dress. I can't remember how many kids she had but it was definitely more than two. After her death, the Monterey paper, The Monterey Peninsula Herald, gave her quite a write-up. She was very important to the history of Cannery Row and Monterey and seemed to be the last of her kind. A couple of years after her death the City realized to contributions made to Cannery Row by Kalisa and they erected a bust of her on the City Property

As I said Kalisa's had many iterations. The first one was a traditional tablecloth on the tables and matching chairs. It would be impossible for me to remember all of the iterations

THE CAMP FOLLOWER

that the restaurant went through, but I do remember some of them.

During the transition between the folk and jazz eras, someone decided that the bar should be flat black to look more jazzy like in the "Village" in New York. In addition it would be nice and sophisticated to have the ceiling wallpapered in newspaper pages. For some reason I couldn't get down to the restaurant when this renovation started. I was quickly introduced to the project when I walked into the building and I heard Kalisa say "John, get a roller or a paintbrush or something". We even blacked out the windows by building the window casements into display boxes that could be seen from the street. It was no time until it was done. During the daylight hours it looked like shit, but at night with a quartet playing jazz, it not only looked good, it sounded good.

The most impressive iteration for the bar was the movie iteration. Kalisa had gone down to Los Angeles and had bought a bunch of movie props from one of the studios. There was a rumor that she had a sugar-daddy for that one. I think some of the things were actual antiques. Anyway there were cadenzas and vases and chairs. The place really looked good.

The transition from folk to jazz had some wonderful benefits. The folk singers had mostly been amateur musicians. With the advent of jazz, the folk singers were replaced by professional musicians wanting to jam with their musician friends on their nights off or after hours. The place even got a reputation for having good jazz.

Someone organized the first Monterey Jazz Festival. These festivals were popular and brought in revenue to the communities. The Monterey Peninsula, or I guess more realistically Carmel, already had the Bach Festival which had been popular for years, but the Jazz Festival would reach more people and could be housed in the Fairgrounds. I was offered a front row box for the first performance; I can't remember who gave me the tickets. I thought it would be fun to invite my folks; they accepted and committed to buying dinner. Then dad suggested that it would be nice if I had a date for the concert. He suggested that his friend's daughter be invited. I didn't know her, but I did know of her father, he was the lettuce king of the Salinas Valley. I wondered if dad was trying to arrange something between us. I drove to Salinas, picked her up at her parent's house, made small talk for awhile and then we drove back to Monterey. We all had an enjoyable dinner and went out to the fairgrounds for the concert. After we had settled into our box, I noticed Kalisa in a box to the right of us. She waved me over, my folks encouraged me to go and say hello, and off I went.

Kalisa told me not to make any plans for the intermission because we were going backstage. She wanted to invite those Jazz greats to play at her restaurant in a jam session. I just looked at her in amazement; this was something that even Kalisa couldn't pull off. The concert started with a full orchestra playing what I remember as Beethoven's Fifth. After a couple of minutes of playing the members of the orchestra put down their instruments got up from their chairs and walked off the stage, and the music was still playing. It took a couple of minutes for the audience to catch on and break into applause. The whole thing was an advertisement for Ampex sound systems; I think the orchestra was the San Francisco Symphony. I've seen similar things later in my life, but the first time was amazing.

THE CAMP FOLLOWER

It was intermission time and Kalisa and I went to the stage door and knocked. The Security Guard opened the door; Kalisa said "I'm Kalisa" and pushed her way into the backstage area. Kalisa is having animated conversations with people like Cal Tjader, Dizzy Gillespie, I think Count Basie, the Modern Jazz Quartet and I don't know who else. Just being in the presence of the world's greatest jazz composers and musicians left me just plain stunned. Kalisa has told them about the jam session and thinks they are all coming to the restaurant. I was stille stunned on the way back to the box. I had just shaken hands with all of the members of the Modern Jazz Quartet and they were my favorite jazz group. I especially liked the theme from "One never knows" which I think was their most popular piece.

After the concert my date, we'll call her the Lettuce Princess suggested that we attend a party in Salinas with some of her friends. I wanted to talk her out of it and tried, unsuccessfully. I wanted to go to the jam session so badly I could taste it. Can you imagine being invited to a jam session with most of the jazz greats playing? The Lettuce Princess didn't seem to have any interest in the world's greatest jam session. So off we go to Salinas and the party. I am introduced to the people at the party and under the circumstances none of them are interesting enough to me for a conversation. After a time, I think it was about an hour or hour and a half later, this guy shows up at the party in a motorcycle jacket and seems to know the Lettuce Princess fairly well. The two of them get into a huddled discussion and then include the hostess of the party. Before I know it the Lettuce Princess and the motorcycle jacket are disappearing into the bedroom closing the door behind them. The party migrates to the other side of the living room and I am left alone on the couch. Now I'm trapped and pissed. If it weren't for the relationship between the Lettuce King and dad, I would have left and gone to the jam session. To keep the family honor, I waited patiently for an excuse to leave. I didn't know sex could take so long for young people. In my mind I think I figured out what was going on, the Lettuce Princess had a long standing relationship with motorcycle jacket that her father didn't approve of, and I was the dupe. They finally emerged from the bedroom, and of course I suggested that I take her home. I do that, get her home and I don't walk her to the front door, she kisses my goodnight and asks if I will be seeing her again. I say sure and under my breath murmur "in your dreams". I take off and go back to Monterey and then to Kalisa's just to find it is dark. Everyone has gone home; I have missed it! I didn't eat domestic lettuce for a long time.

With the Lettuce Princess out of my life, things got back to normal quickly. Listening to jazz at Kalisa's was one of my main things. Kalisa was introducing me to all of the young single women that came into the restaurant. There was a life changing introduction which resulted in another story.

I wandered into Kalisa's one night and Kalisa grabbed me and ushered me to the second floor back room where I think someone with a guitar was playing folk music. She took me to a table with two young ladies sitting there. I was introduced to both of them; one of them was Audrey and the other my future first wife Ingrid. Kalisa made sure that I sat down and started talking to both. Both women were interesting to talk to, Audrey was more Americanized and Ingrid more European. Both of the women were delightful. Ingrid captured my attention because she recently emigrated from Germany. That gave us some common ground and opened the conversation. We dated for awhile and got more intimate until we decided to spend the weekend in Big Sur. At that time I had a '51 Chevy which I decided to rush to its death and treated accordantly. While we were driving from Monterey to Big Sur the car quit running right in front of a motel along Highway One. We checked into a single room and went to the restaurant for dinner. Money was tight because I really hadn't planned for this. We decided that we would share one room. At that time I couldn't guess and I'm sure that Ingrid wondered how I fixed the car so that it would break down in front of that motel. The next morning the car started up immediately which was not my second big surprise of the weekend, but it was a surprise.

After that weekend Ingrid and I became inseparable. Ingrid had moved away from home and was renting a bedroom suite from a very nice lady in Salinas. It just so happens that this lady was a retired school teacher and had taught John Steinbeck in grammar school. She told me some stories about Steinbeck who it turns out was not very studious. Ingrid had her own entrance, bathroom and walk in closet. Her bedroom rental was more like a studio apartment than just a bedroom. I think it was one Saturday afternoon when we were feeling a little frisky and tried to have a little fun in the bedroom. We were in bed when someone knocked on the door. Ingrid asked who it was and the response was Pete. Now Pete was a folk singer who had dated Ingrid before Kalisa introduced us. I was relegated to the closet, nude and no light, until Ingrid could get rid of Pete. After a little while I decided to sit down because I couldn't move my feet around, I couldn't see and didn't want to make any noise. So I sat down right on top of a pair of Ingrid's high heel shoes. That convinced me that certain parts of my body were still alive. Believe it or not I didn't make any noise after the contact with the shoes. It seemed like an eternity since Pete had arrived and it was quite evident that he was trying to mend fences with Ingrid. I don't know how long I sat on those damn shoes, but if you haven't been there don't laugh.

THE RETURN TO MONTEREY

I had been away from Monterey for many years including six year's overseas building things. I had a weekend date in 1982, which was the year I got back to California, and decided that we should go to Monterey. In hadn't been there since the late sixties except for the weekend I was racing there. I wanted to show this girl my Cannery Row, so we went down there. We walked into Kalisa's and I asked the girl behind the counter if Kalisa was around. I didn't know if Kalisa was still alive. The restaurant had become an ice cream parlor by that time. The next thing I knew I heard Kalisa's voice booming from the second floor "John Taylor get your ass up here". My date and I went up to where the old Dining Room was, Kalisa took one look at me with the girl and said "How are Ingrid and the kids?", Kalisa had introduced me to my first wife Ingrid and was sure we probably had kids. I explained that it had been several years since we divorced and this was a new friend, oh, and the kids are fine.

All in all I guess you have to say that my youth was interesting, if not exciting. I got to do things that very few people get to experience and few of those experiences prepared me for a traditional life. I have never been accused of having a traditional life. If it came to a decision between my life and say the characters in "Leave it to Beaver" or the family of "Ozzie and Harriet", I think I would pick my life. In the final analysis I have learned to love the unknown and brinkmanship.

After all of the problems that my parents had, with my mother's drinking and my father's carousing, they stayed married for fifty-nine years ending in his death; with all kinds of bickering and fighting until the end, but they were together. Dad passed away in 1998 of stomach cancer.

I was at their fiftieth anniversary party and I guess that most of the people that attend those things must have a portion of their brain where they store what they know is true. "These people never got along and I'm surprised to be drinking here today!" Everybody at the anniversary party had one hell of a good time and the folks had the best that was offered in a place that they always loved, the Officers Club at the Presidio of San Francisco. Mom passed in 2002, and by God I miss both of them. They gave me an exciting and strange life which I can only say "Thank-you"

Of all the things that were associated with the army, the largest fringe benefit were the medical benefits. The pay was lousy and the folks were always scraping for money. There was a portion of the civilian population who thought we were getting everything for free. Dad had to buy his own uniforms and the army specified the uniform, we paid rent for our living quarters and the discounts at the Post Exchange and Commissary weren't that good. The medical services we got were exceptional. You have to understand that the draft was still in effect and recent medical school graduates were

THE CAMP FOLLOWER

automatically drafted with a rank of Captain. The thing that made it cost effective was that the doctors were on salary, the transportation, if needed, was free and the hospital facilities were the best since they were required to treat battle wounded soldiers. The buildings were old and looked it, that was superficial; the medical equipment was the best. There was no question that mom's back surgery in Heidelberg would be covered by the army because we were in a foreign port. In 1967 mom had a stroke while the folk's were living in Carmel Valley. A call to the hospital at Fort Ord brought an ambulance to the house and mom was transported to the hospital for evaluation. The next morning the diagnoses of a stroke was rendered and she was transported to Letterman General Hospital in the Presidio of San Francisco. Letterman was a regional medical center for the west coast and trauma canter for returning wounded soldiers. A senior neurosurgeon opened mom's brain and removed the blood clot. Her recovery was almost totally successful except she had some lapses of memory until she died. I can remember being worried when I went to visit her and when I walked into the hospital room she looked at me for a couple of minutes, then said and then said "Do I know you, you look familiar?" During the visit I went into the hall which had a great many mutilated soldiers in wheelchairs being moved for treatment. They had just returned from Viet Nam and I can remember thinking how unjust it was for these soldiers to suffer fighting a phony war.

The next experience with the army's medical corps for mom was a bad gall bladder. This happened just prior to the Congress taking away medical benefits from dependents and retirees. Of course Congress kept the benefits for themselves. She was really in pain and they had to do surgery to alleviate that pain. She had this surgeon who she really liked, who had an excellent bedside manner and was a competent surgeon. She was walking down the hall after she recovered and met her surgeon. They started talking and it turns out that he had been relieved of duty. She had been operated on by the Great Impostor. Not only was he not a doctor, but he wasn't even in the army. The authorities wanted mom to file a criminal complaint against him, but she refused, he was better than some of the doctors that had treated her.

After the government had withdrawn the medical benefits from retired military personnel, dad joined a HMO. Before that he was complaining about intestinal pain so I took him to the Naval Hospital where they couldn't find anything wrong of any consequence, although he was told to return if the problem didn't resolve itself. The government then withdrew the benefits and he was forced to rely on the HMO. Ultimately, after about a year he was diagnosed with stomach cancer which was untreatable and he died in two weeks. I often think that he could have had another year if he were treated properly in the military environment.

I had always had an interest in racing sports cars. In what I remember as 1972 I joined the Sports Car Club of America and went to Drivers School at the Riverside Race Track in Southern California. This is of course outside the timeline of this story but it does include Kalisa and Monterey. I had entered the North South Runoff at Laguna Seca in Monterey. My only interest in this story is that someone took a picture of me driving during the race and I have always wanted that photograph. I had bought a Formula Vee race car which was nothing more than a Volkswagen drive train on an open wheeled sled. The engine could pump out in excess of ninety five horsepower and it handled like a larger race car. It was fun and getting it going on a straight away you could get it up to about a hundred miles an hour. Anyway I entered the North South Runoff and prepared the racecar for the event. Believe it or not I had a sponsor for the car. I was in living outside Bakersfield working and getting ready to go to Monterey. My sponsor told me he would take care of all the financial concerns which was one problem that I didn't have to contend with. He let me borrow his Chevy El Camino pickup to tow the racecar over to Monterey. The pickup had a telephone in it, and that was before cellular phones. So I started off for Monterey, there was Tule fog most of the way, visibility was a couple of feet I finally got to Monterey and went over to the hotel where the sponsor told me to meet him. He hadn't arrived yet and wasn't expected. Now I hadn't gotten any money before I left, so here I am broke with a racecar and an event starting tomorrow. This is, of course, before ATM's. So there was only one thing to do and that was to drive over to Kalisa's place and see what I could do to get out of this predicament. I arrived at Kalisa's and talked her into letting me stay in the restaurant over night because I needed some sleep. The deal we struck was that I would take one of her sons to the races with me in the morning. I'm grateful because I didn't want to sleep in the El Camino, it had bucket seats. The next morning we got up and I get cleaned up and put on all of the racing paraphernalia that's required. Fireproof long johns, driving suit fireproof socks, etc, etc. We towed the car out to Laguna Seca got into the pit and waited. I went out and practiced for a couple of laps, then came back in. Everything seemed to be alright with the car. It was time to start the race; we all got into formation for the start. I think we only needed one lap to start the race.

As soon as I hit the throttle hard I knew something was wrong. The car was mishandling to the extreme, it took me a couple of laps to realize that the car's chassis had not been aligned and I was going into turns almost sideways. I couldn't make the car maneuver through a turn at any speed. That's where the picture comes in. Turn nine at that time was a left hand turn at over ninety degrees. The car wouldn't even respond in that turn even though the speed going through the turn was about fifteen miles an hour. That's where the photographer was taking his pictures. He pointed the camera directly into my face and took the picture. I'm sure that the expression on my face was sheer terror and since I never had a picture of me racing, I thought that would be the perfect picture to hang on my wall. I crashed the car a couple of laps later.

Would you like to see your manuscript become a book?

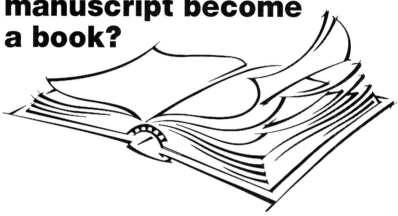

If you are interested in becoming a PublishAmerica author, please submit your manuscript for possible publication to us at:

acquisitions@publishamerica.com

You may also mail in your manuscript to:

**PublishAmerica
PO Box 151
Frederick, MD 21705**

www.publishamerica.com

CPSIA information can be obtained at www.ICGtesting.com
262137BV00001B/15/P